SMART BRAND

EASY-TO-USE BUSINESS SOLUTIONS FOR ENTREPRENEURS AND INFLUENCERS, CREATING YOUR AUDIENCE THROUGH SOCIAL MEDIA MARKETING

© Copyright 2020 by ProBusiness Publishing
All rights reserved.

This document is geared towards providing exact and reliable information with regards to the topic and issue covered. The publication is sold with the idea that the publisher is not required to render accounting, officially permitted, or otherwise, qualified services. If advice is necessary, legal or professional, a practiced individual in the profession should be ordered.

- From a Declaration of Principles which was accepted and approved equally by a Committee of the American Bar Association and a Committee of Publishers and Associations.

In no way is it legal to reproduce, duplicate, or transmit any part of this document in either electronic means or in printed format. Recording of this publication is strictly prohibited and any storage of this document is not allowed unless with written permission from the publisher. All rights reserved.

The information provided herein is stated to be truthful and consistent, in that any liability, in terms of inattention or otherwise, by any usage or abuse of any policies, processes, or directions contained within is the solitary and utter responsibility of the recipient reader. Under no circumstances will any legal responsibility or blame be held against the publisher for any reparation, damages, or monetary loss due to the information herein, either directly or indirectly.

Respective authors own all copyrights not held by the publisher.

The information herein is offered for informational purposes solely, and is universal as so. The presentation of the information is without contract or any type of guarantee assurance.

The trademarks that are used are without any consent, and the publication of the trademark is without permission or backing by the trademark owner. All trademarks and brands within this book are for clarifying purposes only and are the owned by the owners themselves, not affiliated with this document

Page left intentionally blank

TABLE OF CONTENTS

INTRODUCTION 5
    Understanding Social Media 6
    How to become a social media guru? 23
CHAPTER TWO 467
    Identify your target audience 467
    Create a Story Brand framework 66
CHAPTER THREE 845
    Mastering social marketing spectrum 845
    Scaling up your digital business 978
CHAPTER FOUR 109
    Generate solid profit incomes 109
    Make yourself a renowned social media icon 121
CONCLUSION 129

INTRODUCTION

Product owner's expertise will make digital connections with physical products, enabling brands to fundamentally change consumer experience and product lifecycles. Enhanced item personalization brings to the popular branded items a whole new engagement model and incomparable value.

Personal branding is usually represented both in a positive and active way; it communicates what you think is the best about the data your particular operating system continuously processes through visual, auditory, and kinesthetic formats. Branding is used to define the unique combination of your tangible and intangible items (social style) and how you use your contact channels to manifest them.

Branding can take the gamut of ignorance and brash to the courageous, but it ultimately helps you to realize more clearly and honestly who you are. It explains why you can have friends who are connected with you, but who are very different.

Keep an emphasis on personal integrity at the core of your brand mix. You help avoid that your marks are faddish or total imitations of those you socialize with, admire, or favor with. Your brands should clearly understand the values you feel comfortable transmitting publicly.

This is essential to know that it is necessary to identify (visually), explain (verbally), and (physically) you in simple terms known as word images that you get clarification on your products.

If you can communicate your preference of descriptors to a friend verbally and how they best represent who you are, you have come to understand that all of us have more than one dimension. It is healthy and purposeful for each and every one of us to continually develop and sometimes even reinvent ourselves. When we can find acceptance, our friendships and relationships can grow more meaningfully. Sadly, socio-economic influences, fears, restrictions, and other opinions can prevent us from traveling to discover ourselves.

The goals to identify, verbalize, and live your brands are to improve and experience healthy relationships with others. Your brands help like-minded people to recognize 'you' and try to establish a mutual connection and initiate or react to it.

Understanding Social Media

As the owner of small business, you may also have heard others talk of social media marketing and not fully comprehend what was being discussed, merely pushing it to another mode or a collection of mood words thrown by professional manufacturers. But this marketing seems here to remain, and the positive thing is that it's actually exceptionally easily understandable, and then you can also put yourself in a few strategies.

Social media platforms are websites that connect people to family and friends and, sometimes, strangers who share common interests. Although most individuals use these platforms to stay in touch with their family members, marketing experts realize that these sites are indeed a great way to keep businesses in contact with their customers and to present them with new ones. As a small business owner, you can show your company and your products the same way other people can show their new kitten or equipment for an evening out. Social media marketing tries to interact with and interact with your customers.

Many different social media sites, such as Facebook, Twitter, LinkedIn, and Pinterest, have various features. Some sites may be more appropriate for some companies than others. You can choose to maintain a broad site portfolio (many of which can be easily connected to each other) or focus your attention on the ones that suit your company best. If you wish to maintain an extensive portfolio, it is best to hire a social media marketing expert to help you, as it might take time to remain active on each of these sites. If you want to run your own social network, experts advise you to monitor social media content and to speak to your followers for at least 30 minutes a day.

Interactions can be as accessible as the positive comments of a fan and thanks to them to a quick public. While it may seem paradoxical because you're a graphical being behind a computer screen, even the least contact and appreciation you offer fans will lead to a human face for your business that enhances your public image. In fact, scientists have found that some people have the same rush of endorphins when a celebration acknowledges Twitter to them as they have chocolate to make them feel the same kind of unique and receive a message from a company that they like.

The point of this advertisement is to look friendly while subtly promoting your brand name and your goods by helping to increase the brand's exposure. It is essentially an online way to network with customers, but you should usually do soft selling rather than hard-selling so that you do not alienate people.

For several global events around the world, social media and social networking are influential. And many people have this misunderstanding that these two are the same and can be used interchangeably. Knowing the difference between Social Media and Social Networking helps you to better understand how you can use it for your brand and business and how you can position your company in the future. Surely these two aren't the same. Here are some comparisons of the two in order to remove your confusion.

Social networking is, by definition, a tool for distributing or exchanging information with a broad audience. Everyone has the opportunity to create and distribute their own. It's a channel of communication more likely. It is not a place to visit and leave; it is a system that distributes information to others. Social networking is hard work and can take a lot of time in terms of timely response. It certainly isn't a sprint, but a marathon. You have no hope of automating individual interactions unless you are a renowned organization and have successfully developed a brand. You are not allowed for personal or business gain to distort or exploit comments. Followers in construction don't just happen immediately. So if word spreads by accident about your unethical activities, you will be in deep trouble so your PR will be affected.

Social networking, on the other hand, is a device and an act of interaction. It is where people meet, share mutual values, and build relationships across the community. Here's two-way communication. People gather to join others in accordance with the subject, subject, or atmosphere. They share their experiences and backgrounds in this respect. And relationships are developed through this.

Conversations between you and the people you choose to connect with are more productive, more meaningful, and more personal because there is direct communication. Your network will undoubtedly grow as you meet and contact other people in the community. Social networking can be used to promote your new business or blog in comparison to social media. You should tell anyone you meet about it and think about how you can make it a success. These people will probably soon become your loyal fans. So it's worth investing your time in this one.

One thing these two have in popular is they both based on marketing viral to succeed. Both are increasing the importance of a company. The virus depends on the methods used. Like, for example, if the content becomes viral, more people are paying attention to it while at the same time increasing your online traffic. This is how social media helps people connect, and social networking is responsible for improving this connection. The main reason many people still use these two practices is that they get common interests, causes, and passions, and want to build up and strengthen relationships with each other over time.

To make your business more successful, it is essential to know and understand that while they overlap sometimes, they certainly aren't the same, and each one plays a vital role in your business. Through using their features entirely, you become more active.

WHAT DOES SOCIAL MEDIA DO AND WHY SHOULD YOU CARE?

If you are the same as many, you look at today's young people who continually tap their smartphone touchpad and wonder: "What do they have to say and for whom?!" Then you're discounting all social media and brushing off instant global connectivity and the whole digital universe of the 21st century with Scrooge-like "harrumph!" You only put the operation of your corporation or rule behind the others.

All right, so you don't have to jump into social media and start posting what you do in every minute around the world, but at least you ought to understand what it is about so that you can use it if you want or know how it is applied in litigation.

Obviously, this book will not provide legal advice or form a legal relationship with the reader; it is intended only to provide general information about important social media issues and their effect on current business and legal practices.

What really is social media?

By the 2012 summer, Americans spent approximately one hundred and twenty billion minutes on social media a month, up from eighty-eight billion a year earlier. This represents up to 30% with all time spent on the internet. More than six hundred million people are now using Facebook, and over half of all Americans are social media.

The affordability and popularity of smartphones also significantly increases mobile use. The truth is that the application is up, and you can see it around you and hear it daily. So, it's here to stay for better or worse.

Okay, so you know you can no longer ignore that, but you don't yet know that you need it or that you want to use it and wonder what it really is. In order to divide this information briefly, it can be divided into two broader groups, (i) websites hosting content created by users, like videos, photos, text posts, and (ii) websites that replicate content as well as provide enhanced visibility on the internet.

There are some of the most frequently used or "older" pages under the first group, which are over five years old, such as LinkedIn, Facebook, YouTube, Twitter, and Google+ for example, and other maybe less known or "newer" sites such as Ezine, Pinterest, Delicious, Slideshare, Squidoo, About.me. Even in the second group, there are older sites like Linkedin, Tweet Deck, Hootsuite, and newer sites like Reddit, Sharehaulic, or StumbleUpon.

Which are the advantages and uses of social media?

Okay, now you know what social media is, and you still wonder how it affects you. One very fascinating aspect of social media is the apparent mixture of legitimacy and exposure. If thousands of people embrace, for example, what an actor or actress says in social media or do it in a certain way, it indicates that those who are famous in social media automatically have legitimacy with their attractive crowds. It's a weird world where the profits of a shop will increase simply because of the social media posts of a reality television show star, but that's the world in which we live today and the world you must recognize because it affects your company and that of your customers.

And Why You Would Know-Litigation Social Media

So, when you get to the heart of the issue, you know social media, you use it or are at least willing to use it, so how do you incorporate it in litigation? First of all, you might already know the e-discovery components were included in the Florida Civil Procedure Rules on 1 September 2012. This means that electronic information, including e-mails, is now discoverable in Florida in civil lawsuits.

While the Federal case law on the subject is growing, a recent decision of the Virginia State Court accepted the lawyer with more than $500,000 for allowing his client to delete posts and images from social media platforms related to the case. The worst thing is that the prosecutor was guided not by the lawyer but by a paralegal, but the Court found that the attorney was aware of that and allowed it. While this may be an extreme case, the day is not far off when Florida has decisions in this regard.

I would like to present a theory to explain how social media impacts litigation and e-discovery. Let's take a client who claims he or she will no longer be able to lift, bend, or whatever. This person, or even a friend of that person, takes pictures of him or her skiing during the litigation and has a great time in the hot tub near the slopes. If you defend the case, these photos make your customer very happy. Possibly they won't if you try the case. As you can see, social media understanding and how to ethically get those posts are now a relevant and essential part of Florida's law practice.

In addition to receiving electronic evidence, including these communications, parties and their counsel are now obligated to act in advance, by means of mechanisms such as litigation holdings. Florida lawyers must also be aware of the liabilities of their customers for not preserving ESI, whether requested or, in some cases, not advised. For more information, please visit the two featured e-discovery videos on my homepage.

In addition, Florida's lawyers and entrepreneurs are now unable to avoid social media. Though you do not want to tell the world what you think of a film that you have just seen through these messages, you must at least understand what social media basics are and how it can impact a legal case in which you engage or engage later on.

Because companies, in particular, are continually trying to store all their data electronically, and people live in the modern world of social media, social media can no longer be ignored. It's not as easy as you probably thought, and once you try it, you can develop comfort and even embrace it.

Social medieval trends for the future.

New social media platforms emerge without notice in contemporary times. This makes it difficult for someone to decide which platform their time, resources, and effort should be dedicated to. It is, therefore, prudent to take stock of the future of social networks and prepare how to participate profitably. But let's first reply to the question most asked...

Do I need professional social media marketing services?

With most businesses combining their social media strategy with quality content and improving results, one can definitely conclude that social networks are here and that any company would probably have the best advertising strategies today.

Social media have a measurable effect on referral traffic, lead generation, and higher revenues. In fact, this has led some companies to lift social media roles from their regular employees and pass them on to qualified professionals.

With an outstanding social media strategy, businesses can effectively build brand awareness, increase circulation through many site hits, improve customer loyalty and trust, and gain access to a broader target market.

Focus on social media avenues

Google + Goes to be a critical social media player

Google+ is the second-largest network with many active monthly Facebook users. This means that any business that is serious about their presence in social media cannot overlook Google+. This also gives Google a more reliable way to access personal information of its users, for example, profiles and location.

This makes Google+ a significant player in Google's main social signals and SEO scheme because it leads to a more customized search experience. Google+ is very substantial as it is related to Google Authorship, another main component of the search ranking algorithm.

Enhanced use of image and video content

In 2013, a change was made from text to image and video marketing. Well, the influence of visual content cannot be diminished, and this creates not only social networking sites, such as Pinterest, a network that others view but also an excellent marketing tool for any retailer.

Tumblr, Path, Mobli, and Slideshare are other image-based networks that are expected to expand. In this case, businesses should understand whether they can share their photos further when shared on their blogs or websites if they want to benefit from the marketing of social media.

Increased image and video sharing are also driven by the appearance of micro video applications such as Twitter's Vine and Instagram's video-sharing feature. It actually indicates that we will share videos up to 3-15 seconds in real-time, like with Instagram. Vine allows users to share videos that can be created and shared from a smartphone for 6 seconds.

An interesting trend to see is how morsel-sized content could change the game in video and image marketing.

Concentrate on business growth LinkedIn

This is the number one technical, social networking site. You can think that LinkedIn is sitting on his heels. Nonetheless, this is becoming the next networking platform, with over one million users to see businesses searching for significant talents in all fields and producing content. This allows any severe marketer to "talk" in advance and reap the tremendous advantages until the network gathers traction.

THE TWITTERVERSE, TWITTER, AND TWEEPLE

Inextricably linked appears social media, Twitter, social media marketing, and Internet marketing! This is the first Twitter tool, application, and its use in a purely social and marketing context. This is the beginning of a series. It is my hope that by the conclusion of this show, a whole new range of tools and apps will be open to you, and that you will understand the true essence of Twitter and the way it blends into the Internet marketing environment.

The global community is the flutter ahead of Twitter, and it's the honeymoon of social media and the whole Internet. A host of Twitter tools and software are open to both novices and experts. Or should I say ' guru and newbie,' both? Interestingly, the social media jargon and the lexicon of all Internet marketing seem to have accepted this rather extensive use of the term guru. Twitter, however, is an undeniable hit and a social media site that, in the opinion of this author, has not yet reached its full potential. The numbers of apps, software, websites, posts, forums, marketing campaigns, and advertising opportunities are utterly stunning. Whilst this focuses on the most widely utilized and popular Twitter usage platforms, Twitter single and/or multiple ones, subsequent will reveal several remarkably innovative tools that are just starting to emerge and take their place in what some call the Twitter-verse!

Twitter as a Platform for Stand Alone

Naturally, our first application or platform, Twitter itself, is the most obvious. Twitter offers an impressive array of features for all the alternative tools and applications without ever leaving the nest. Now we are all aware of the 140-character limit, and although we have an app that allows the limit to double, most of us are comfortable using 140 characters, using contractions, abbreviations, and other twitter-Esque codes, which enables us to get our messages or "tweets" to each other.

Trend

"Trending Themes" is just a resource available without ever leaving the front page. The tool "Trending Themes" allows one to see the most common topics at a glance. Interestingly, at least directly, most items have very little to do with Internet marketing. The search feature, usually found in the side-panel, at least on the most fundamental, traditional page, allows Twitterers or Tweeple to type in any keyword, depending on who you listen to and whether or not you follow a person, you immediately get popular tweets that are important to that keyword. There are a number of applications using different search methods and various Twitter search engines, but most Tweeples are more than suited to the straightforward search application!

The page of the profile

The profile page allows a person or individual to see what other Twitterers have been tweeting about and to refresh their minds about their own tweets at a glance. It also provides a name, location, web address, and a short biography of the individual, in most cases. The profile page also contains the number of followers and those followed by the user. Eventually, the profile page also displays the number of notifications for any person and the behavior of the user, in a definite sense, and the last tweet. With the information on this page, you can tell what people concentrate on, how frequently and at whatever time of day or night, and how many and whom they follow on Twitter and tweets, and vice versa. In reality, this is a lot of knowledge and can be very helpful when deciding whether to follow or not.

Search for people

The next tool offered by Twitter is "Find People." Ironically, this method has many features, in addition to simply finding a single person. Like the search application, the "Find People" tool can be used to find every person who has mentioned a particular keyword and who has spoken about it. Therefore, Tweeple can see who those people tweet to and if those Twitters tweet to others on the same subject, go deep into the list of followers and records of others. The keywords can vary from back pain to the Iranian elections, and the results are identical and recognize potential followers, Tweeple, with common interests. With this information, you can decide whether to follow someone, offer an idea to help them, or perhaps answer a question, comment on an observation made, and thus enhance "your brand" on twitter verse.

Connections and configurations

Ultimately, the feature 'Connections' inside 'Settings' is one of the newest apps, or at least the one which has been improved by the social media trend, far later on. Twitter introduced numerous tools and applications that not only boost your search capabilities but also enable you to easily follow others and to unfold rapidly. Most of the apps and resources in "Connections" have been developed to enhance the ability to connect with other Tweeples, to track current trends and to publicize yourself and services in twitter verse.

Will you pay for Twitter?

Twitter stormed the World. Social media is the sweetheart of the Internet and social media marketing that everyone reaches out to. Social media marketing, as previously stated, may actually be an oxymoron. Interestingly, with all its recent press and publicity, the social web is often somewhat confusing, perhaps a paradox. While many believe that there's richness in social media, particularly Twitter, the jury still thinks it's out. Ploked has just confirmed that Twitter's $3 million sales announcement shows that the social media giant is now a legitimate marketing tool.

The Question of $3,000,000!

We will also take some time to analyse the state of social media and try to make specific claims such as those made by Ploked, Mashable, and others. And that's basically the issue of the 3 million dollars, isn't it, "Does the social media pay?" and beyond that: "Does Twitter pay?" In the opinion of this journalist, though plausible, the knowledge is not definitive and could be misleading.

The revealed Internet Marketing Quest and The Last Internet Image are the culmination of a year-long "Second Ph.D.," immersion in all aspects of Internet Marketing. After more than 30 years of technology, Web marketing, and social media and marketing have posed a fascinating challenge.

MAKING SOCIAL MEDIA WORK FOR YOUR SMALL BUSINESS

As a corporate owner, you realize how dangerous social media is to your business' success. You have learned what you need to know to make social media work for you. Yet you think it's not enough. What must you do? What must you do?

Allow good use of social media for your company.

If you have a small company, there are some variations in the approach you need to take with social media. Social media channels and the way you work them isn't "one size fits everybody." The social media platforms you use and how you use these networks for the desired effect are bound to be different for you than for other business owners. One thing you should remember always is that social media works for you. You can find out how to make it function as well as possible.

By principle, you can agree that social media is a useful marketing tool and can make the best use of it. However, you're not going to get very far without a deep understanding of how to make it work for you and your business. You won't achieve the results you're looking for if you don't get too far.

You must make sure your social media marketing strategy is sound, and you understand precisely where you are doing so before you can get involved in social media. Before that, you will see what you are doing and know what you are failing and what you have to change to produce more favorable results.

You can do (or not) those things and don't know what they are. You can't fix them if you haven't found them.

The concept of quality versus quantity is fundamental. Value versus quantity. If you collect 10,000 fans and followers but interact with only 50 of them, what do you actually gain by having 10,000? If people passed you on the street, you wouldn't know the remaining fans and followers. So, what interest do you really have? You can focus much more on the quality of your connections and ensure that these interactions advance your relationships. This is really important for you to bear in mind that you will continue to communicate with these people if you really want your relationship to advance. You can comment on what you say, ask questions, ask for your views, ask them for your content, etc. Another important thing is to share your story. That's how you can communicate personally / emotionally with the other guy. If you appeal to their feelings, they will respond to you and want to keep engaging more closely with you.

Don't forget analysis: gathering data from your interactions with social media may sound like a waste of time, but it may be more relevant than you know. If you pay attention to measurements, you will see what you do well and what you don't work for. You will describe these essential aspects of your social media marketing activities if you are able to recognize what is not working. In this case, information is definitely power. The critical aspects of your attempts to promote your social network are not only your interactions but also the way you communicate. You want to interact as efficiently as you can and must commit yourself to spend uninterrupted time and effort every week on your social media marketing strategy. You're going to see that it pays off. But remember that it may take you a little time to see the results. Don't assume that these outcomes should be obtained. You have to be very careful.

Show other people what you and your business worth: you build relationships with other people when interacting through social media online. You can't really connect with the other person without these qualities. Part of that is the belief that the other person will understand why engaging with you is worthwhile. If you can't explain (prove to them) why they should connect with you (and keep connecting), the relationship won't go any further. All this goes back to the concept of WIIFM (What's in it for me?). In other words, only if you are able to fix the problems is of interest to the other person. Also, remember to keep your messages clear, succinct, and up to date. The other person will greatly appreciate it.

Don't squeeze away your uniqueness: it is essential for you to check your networks of social media periodically. What may have been meaningful at first can no longer be significant. If you reach this conclusion, you can eliminate some channels and replace them with others that work better for you and your company. You have to review every aspect of these profiles when you analyze your social media profiles. You will typically find something to tweak that will eventually make a difference. It's usually a productive thing to refresh what you have.

Recognizing that your strategy for social media marketing is yours alone: it is never a good idea to assume that your plan of social media marketing fits in a circular pitch. That's never going to be the case. Your social media marketing strategy is unique to your business, and ultimately you want people to buy what you are selling. If you offer products and/or services that others can get anywhere, what do they need? It is likely that another person can sell what appears to be the same thing you offer for less money. Remember, however, that on the surface, it only seems like that. It is your job to explain why your offerings are better.

Concluding

You may not realize that you miss some incredible marketing opportunities for social media. It is essential to be mindful of what you're doing to make sure you recognize to repair what doesn't work. If you work with your small company on social media, you will have the same effect as larger businesses. You just have to work out how to do it effectively. It's also important to remember that it doesn't mean you can't make a big bang just because you may have limited resources! You can certainly. That is the only way you will allow your company to proceed. Standing still is the same as reversing.

How to become a social media guru?

Social networking is an inclusive term, and not a cup of tea is becoming a pioneer in the region. You must have the right experience and ability to master it. Many experts will help you achieve your destination on social media.

Over a long time, we have seen tremendous improvements in technology, from fans to A.C., tapes to aqua guards, and computers to laptops. Nobody can dissipate in some way just one day without benefiting from significant generational changes. The same is true of the newspapers. Human beings have endured the listening to radios, the reading to papers, and the watching of television tremendously, and now the time for users of social media is significantly increased.

Parents had to draw their children inside the house at one age, and now is the period when they have to take them out. It has managed to take over all aspects of the media. Nevertheless, it is definitely not limited to children and young people. This is helpful to marketing managers, companies, marketers, and everybody else. Follow the following points, and no one will stop you from being an expert in social media:

As a king of the company (Expert):

Everybody uses it today. Anyone in it can open a profile. The confusion occurs when someone thinks that this will make them a king of social media. Social media is a vast field, and it is so difficult to master it. Indeed, the concept is simple, but many things have to be learned. You have to know them inside of the field, only then you can manage it and start your business on different platforms.

Identify your market objective:

You have gained and mastered expertise in the field, and the second stage is the identification of your target market. So, before you start such a media campaign, you have to recognize which people are taking care of your business? You can aim your campaign to attract particularly this group of customers you have chosen. You found this out. Various groups of people may be targeted simultaneously. The next step is to design your strategy so that more and more people can attract you.

Which is your bid of value for your prospect?

Offer them the services they want after knowing your target audiences. Choose the specific services you want to offer your customers. Create a list of deals you can give your customers; this will allow them to visit more and more potential customers at the same time. You are also incredibly flexible in selecting services, depending on the type of business you operate.

Discuss quality and customer satisfaction:

Inform your customers about the quality of your products. The main goal of every company is customer satisfaction. Let your company's products and services meet and outshine customer expectations. Provide your clients with the latest consumer goods to ensure the highest quality and customer satisfaction.

Speak about the profession 's best breed:

Select the best class platforms to market your product. There are many social media sites on which your industry can be promoted according to the type of sector. The different websites of social media are:

Facebook:

Facebook is the best and most excellent way to promote your company online. Although it is widely regarded as a personal use site for more and more adults, it will definitely be the next most extensive B2B networking and marketing tool.

Twitter:

Twitter is the most accessible platform for a company to support. You can find people with similar interests and connect and communicate with them.

LinkedIn:

LinkedIn is a platform for all small, medium-sized, and large companies. It is used to build a strong relationship and to provide feedback and insights into the company and its services.

YouTube:

YouTube is the main forum for video marketing. Today more and more people are drawn to innovative videos, and using YouTube is the most advanced technology to support your business.

Free Blogger:

Blogging is an excellent and the best way to connect and talk to people about your business or its services. Blogs must be updated periodically.

Squidoo:

The Squidoo is an excellent website for content sharing that can help you attract your target customers.

Engage your customers in your talk:

The best way to use this media is to follow a two-way street. Companies can discuss this directly with their customers. Your clients should offer suggestions and feedback that can be worked on. You can also join a number of industries and communities and interact with specialists for anything you want to know about your arena.

Automated:

You can save a lot of time by automating your social media activity. After all, you have a business to work with. There are numerous automation platforms to automate networking activities: Twitter, Blabber, CoTweet, HootSuite.

Monitor:

Social media is a way for you, your business, your products, and services to market. The next step is to know how successful your social media business is. It can be hard to monitor how your performance is done across the Internet. With powerful tools like Google Analytics, the presentation and results of the company can be controlled through many social media platforms.

Would you like to change your strategy?

Social networking is an unfailing tactic. It made many small businesses well-known and well-known. Where there is a 90 % chance of social media success, it still has a 10% chance of not succeeding. Planning B will also be able to prevent any delays. Maintaining your alternatives ready can help your company not to go down.

Nowadays, the internet is used for all and by everyone, so that the status of internet marketing guru is not attainable. Although competition is increasing in network marketing, there are opportunities for all those who are willing to take a few essential steps in the game of the internet.

Internet marketing is only one more way to promote web-based products or services. You can do this in conjunction with network marketing. Every day, you view online ads through banners, ad blocking, and blogs. Internet Marketing Gurus know that the main aim of marketing is to catch the attention of your audience. With the right techniques in place, a business will be built. That is the target. So, how do you take care of yourself?

Read the book

Without absorbing all information, they could, Internet marketing gurus did not become Gurus. Read topics that help you create a blog or other issues with your business, like HTML code, that can help you develop better ideas about your marketing strategy. Make sure you understand what you read and use what you know to help draw customers to your product or service in this way.

Become active with people like you

When in a dark place, only because you have a screen, it would be easy to get an hermitage, internet marketing gurus do not use a phone. Begin to become active with local groups with people like minds who have similar visions. If you have no local group, create one. You should join a local Toastmaster community to practice the skills of your public speaking if you want to talk to your network marketing team. Only be around like caring people.

Be One Step Forward

Gurus selling the Internet are not waiting for creativity. You build it, or you know the new and best tools and knowledge before it becomes a phenomenon. Some don't even know how to start using so many different online resources, but understanding how to work with your specific internet marketing or network marketing company is essential. For example, the use of social media sites to market business is something that is currently becoming a huge trend, but the Internet marketing guru used social media a few years ago before all the rage.

Test Split

Split testing is something we just saw the real internet marketing gurus doing. In essence, split tests are used as a "power" topic to find something productive for you while searching for better methods. Whether you have a capture page and test various colors or fonts to replace images and your PPC ads, split testing can be an excellent way to make your good "great."

Create a free product

Not all internet marketing guru are geniuses, but I can guarantee that they all have something free. This can be a free newsletter, instruction, video training, or it can be useful and make a DVD. It has been shown that people like to be safe. It draws people like flies to sweetheart by using something of value (the value being the main word). The trick is to get people attracted to whatever you sell. If you give someone something free of charge, they will most likely examine your actual product or offer in greater detail.

Basically, the online marketing guru is not rocket science. You are guaranteed to get your guru status in no time by following these five easy steps and creating an enormous online Empire along the way.

YOUR BUSINESS AND SOCIAL MEDIA

Avoid treating technology and social media as passive distributors. There are some fantastic stories of people who have gone from rag to riches with these new inventions to pave the way for a lot of prosperity. Yes, if you use these fantastic new kinds of communication properly, you can have advanced combustion of your success.

The likely hood that any business with comparable outcomes is as probable as anyone on the planet receives the lottery system. See this modern technology for what it really is, just supplementary resources that help and improve your networking and marketing activities, allowing you and your business to make full use of social media and the Internet.

Therefore, any business seeking to thrive in the new global marketplace must incorporate into its activities, both targeted social media and Internet optimization strategies. The goal is to look at these fantastic modern devices and see what they really are. They're not the one-stop, fast-moving solution every contractor is searching for to fix all their marketing and networking problems. They are truly incredible tools that can speed up and multiply someone's networking and marketing campaigns when properly used.

When can I use this modern technology?

If you dip your toe once a week into the social networking sites arena and add a web site, the phone will indeed not ring and open the borders as orders just go through the door. These are powerful additional tools that support your marketing and networking efforts. They will never be the full marketing and networking one-stop-shop. The secret of making this strategy work for you is to keep in mind that business fundamentals have not changed. People still purchase from companies they know, like, trust, and offer them or their companies the best value.

In developing your social media and internet strategy, your goal is to use the new technology to help you get the right people to the right place, who want to know, like and trust you and your product and service that you sell.

Social media understanding as a business tool
The way companies can connect and interact with their markets has been transformed by social media. Consumers are now more likely to connect and receive nearly immediate feedback from any product or service provider. You want to know that business is listening to you and that you meet your needs exactly how you want them to be met.

This new technology has opened up a whole new way of doing business and provides companies with an excellent tool for marketing their products and services. It also provides customers with a forum and allows them to demand quality goods and services from businesses.

Businesses that will flourish in the coming years will seize this opportunity with both hands and begin to listen to what their markets demand. They provide what the customer needs and ensure that they communicate this very clearly through social media via a targeted marketing strategy.

The challenge facing all businesses at present is for both sides to immerse themselves in social media and join the discussion. This is a terrible tactic, and companies are going to do harm than good through blindly plunging into what they know very little or nothing about. Any corporation wishing to participate in social media should abide by such fundamental business standards.

- Know precisely what your strategy is about.
- Build your plan on the measurement criterion and continuously track your success against all these criteria.
- Devise a plan which outlines your goals and vision clearly
- Monitor your links and clearly outline the intent of using any social media form.
- Tweak your plan and strengthen it until it fulfills your standards.

This new technology is just a unique platform to communicate our message to the people who know, like, and trust our businesses. Social media offers a better or different platform to the traditional methods of marketing like radio, TV, magazines, etc., but the requirements for a successful marketing campaign are necessarily the same. Companies must still find ways to get the right consumers to know their market offerings, like them, and value them in their target markets.

Start

The first step is to engage in social media education and what it offers. This is simple and starts with searching the internet by typing in Google the question you would like to answer. Every question you have about social media and how to use it in your organization can be solved conveniently on the internet. Stay clear and avoid the myriad offers of immediate success and spend millions only 30 minutes a day on the Internet or on social media.

If you understand how social media can benefit your business and how to develop your social media strategy. You can employ a skilled social media coach to help you build an effective strategy. We are advised of due diligence. Be very careful about whom you use, as in any business decision. There are countless so-called experts who claim to be part of this new trend.

When you start signing up for TweetBeep updates, and listen to the discussion on your target market, listen to what people might tell about yours or the goods or services of your rival. Note how your competitors communicate with the market and how they receive feedback on the market. It helps you to determine how your message and communication is placed in your target market.

This digital media medium is a modern and exciting interactive communication tool that will propel the company to a new level of success when correctly leveraged.

Using social media to network and promote the business
Avoid the temptation to leap into social media headlong. Throwing all you have to create strong global systems. This is an unnecessary strategy that wastes enormous resources and gets very little or no business opportunity. The entire plan is to raise awareness as to who you and your business are, who don't really care, and would certainly not buy anything you will offer.

Essential business managers are always there, so before you start creating a social media strategy, make sure you first know who your ideal customer is.

Action: Explore the service and product and or identify the ideal customer who needs your product or service. This is the most crucial step in the development of your social media strategy. The next move is to help the tech wizard figure out where these people are on social media sites.

When you have found the forums or sites that hang out those users, the next step is to start connecting with these targets and to regularly communicate valuable information. The way to succeed in using social media to make this targeted group of people aware of, like, and trust you and your company is through commenting on blogs and posts to provide valuable information and engage in relevant conversations with such people. With time, you will be considered the expert, and people will come to you to help you overcome a problem or offer a product or service. When social media is used as an enterprise tool, success is always about giving, caring, sharing, and never taking.

THE GUIDE TO BECOME A SOCIAL MEDIA GURU

It is unquestionable that any organization must be involved in social media. Current consumers' ever-changing expectations allow brands to rapidly think and adjust to remain a step ahead.

The position of a manager of social media attracted the mass generation of socially engaged internet users. It's not hard to. Especially if you think you can get big bucks from posting updates on Facebook.

Being a manager of social media is a kind of comedian. You need to know your audience quickly, and your commitment to them is essential. To achieve this, you must know whether the audience laughs at your witches, and you need to know that in real-time. If you can, you have won the crowd already.

So, how are you going to become a social manager?

Some people will be surprised by the answer. First of all, you must want it. Second, you will love it. Third, you must learn. You must learn it. And even if you tick all those boxes, you should ask yourself, "Am I a social person?" If you answer no, then you probably do not want to be a social media manager.

Let's look at the numbers.

- LinkedIn reveals 57,910 social media admin results
- 71% of users who receive a brand response on social media say they probably recommend the brand to others
- 93 percent of marketers use corporate social media
- 97% of all customers look online for local businesses
- Nearly half (49%) of B2B marketer's location social marketing at the heightened level, followed by the content marketing (39%), mobile (25%) and SEO (26%).
- 25% of the marketing budgets are now spent on content delivery, development, and promotion, on average
- 78% of small enterprises attract new clients via social facilities
- When asked to assess the maturity of your company in the range 1-10, more than half of global business leaders gave their company a ranking of 3 or less.

Nonetheless, the statistics that are most important are:

- Only 12% of those who use social marketing feel that they actually use it.

Being a social media manager brings some key advantages to a freelance environment. The most recognizable thing is your own boss. You decide, and you don't answer anyone. The invoices are submitted, and the policies are set. Heck, if you wanted, you could sit all day in your underpants on the computer.

The other is currency. It's a demand-driven position, but companies still struggle to achieve. Some companies know and appreciate the value of social media for their businesses and are prepared to heavily invest in social media campaigns. You can decide as your own boss, how to set your costs and prices accordingly.

The low barriers to entry are another critical reason. With small start-up costs and plenty of online resources (such as this one!), people can launch a free social management company in a short space of time to quickly reduce their learning curve.

I'm going to tell you my story shortly, but first, let's explore the fundamental skills to become a great manager of social media.

Fundamental competences:

Knowledge of marketing

Some marketing awareness may be helpful, but otherwise, many quality tools can be found online.

Learning Experience
That experience does not need to be restricted to life experiences. Did you manage your own profiles on social media for a while? Do you know how to maintain your personal social accounts effectively and understand what customers expect?

Sociable

When you are not a sociable person, someone who does not like to communicate much and who doesn't really like it, then it's just not for you to be a social media manager. Indeed, you can hide for a while behind a keyword and monitor, but usually, clients want to meet, talk on a phone, and have Skype meetings at some moment.

Management of the project

You don't need to have a certificate of Prince2, but you have to manage your projects and your time well. It is typical for managers of social media to work with multiple customers at any time. It is essential to keep track of things so that it does not become overwhelming.

Technology

Social media is available online. You must, therefore, have a certain degree of computer literacy. Keen social technology awareness will improve your services and ensure that you keep up with current social trends and innovations.

Interpersonal competencies:

interaction

It goes with no need for strong communication skills if you are going to represent a company and interact with its customers.

Personality

Organizations tend not to employ people without any personality for their brand. They or their audiences do not resonate well with them.

Responsibility

Just imagine whether one of your social tasks focused mainly on customer service, and you did not answer customer complaints or requests for weeks. People online want instant answers. If you can meet these needs, your customer (and you!) can stand well.

Company entrepreneurship

To become a freelance social media boss, you have to be a self-starter. You should be prepared to go a little further and take some financial risks along the way. If in a month you don't get a job that pays enough, how does that affect you?

Multiple tasks
A famous social media guru should be able to perform a wide variety of assignments effectively.

Company
When providing social media management services, you should always be very well organized. Use every kind of existing technique such as calendars, whiteboards, and task lists to organize yourself. Use many online organizational tools, like Thunderbird, to access all of the e-mail in one place, Dropbox to simple documents sharing with customers and also bookmarks to monitor all websites visited frequently.

Strategic Pension
To be able to think about promotions before they occur and to think outside the box when needed are significant advantages as a social media manager. Customers continue to want to learn how they can do it before

they let them do it so that a straightforward and succinct plan can be delivered.

Flexible (traveling)

Unlike popular belief, a freelance social media manager sometimes has to leave his office! If this is an issue for you, consider beginning another career. Almost every major project involves multiple meetings with the customer. You should be able to pitch correctly, because before you are hired, you may be required to sell your services face to face too. You can even choose to do in-house work.

Wider capabilities:

Collection of copies

Any good manager of social media is a great blogger. Writing forms the basis for many aspects of online marketing, be it the creation of advertising, writing blogs, interactions with customers, writing copies of sales, or writing press releases.

Design of graphics

Virtually every social media platform can customize the interface as well as incorporate your branding. When you are sharp with Photoshop (or similar design software), you can offer them as part of your social media package. Similarly, for a social media manager, the production of content such as banners, infographics, or images is standard practice.

Advertising

Each social media manager should have sound advertising knowledge. Whether (PPC) Pay-Per-Click advertising or banner ads, the ins, and outs of each discipline and how to optimize each format should be understood.

PR

Public relations are closely linked to social media marketing, which includes both handling the distribution of information between a corporation and the public. You may not need to have a profound knowledge of PR because it is generally managed by more prominent brands that have an investor, stakeholder, or public interest in maintaining a particular view.

Statistical Statistics

Everything should be measured in marketing. You will calculate and review your social media success regularly and generate reports for your customers to demonstrate your importance.

SEO

Ultimately, understanding how social media affects the optimization of search engines will improve campaign performance. In 2012, Google conducted an average of 5,134,000,000 searches every day. If you think your social interactions don't matter to SEO, think again.

Traditional commercialization

Although you generally do not participate in conventional marketing practices while taking on the role of social media management, you should understand how both marketing forms affect each other and how each of them can be best used to add to the other.

Editing of video

This may be the least used of your broader skills, but it can nevertheless help you in your social marketing position. You have some customers that needed presentations or demonstration videos to be edited before their social media campaigns were used. You are certainly not an expert, but with a reasonable level of knowledge of Windows Movie

Creation (or video editing Application), this video file can be transformed from the camera into a lovely, YouTube-ready video.

Also, when you have all the skills to become a social media professional, you have room to develop your services with various marketing resources and apps. We will recapture two different software pieces quickly, which can help you to become a great social media manager:

- Hootsuite: write a comprehensive overview of Hootsuite on a blog, including a video tutorial that will contain all the information you need to learn on Hootsuite.

- BuzzBundle: these are some of the most preferred and respected apps ever used. Use it mainly to find keywords about content subjects from a wide variety of blogs, forums, and social websites and transmit all of this information to an interface.

What you're going to expect to do ...

So, what is a social media manager doing? As you can probably guess, the position of a social media manager is different. This is not a case of "Ok, I post Facebook updates." There are several general tasks that social media managers are supposed to perform:

Plan

You will be required to develop campaigns and platforms that meet your business goals. You will create action plans, content calendars, metrics, and KPIs, undertake different research activities, and conduct various analytical methods.

Creation of Content

Content provides the basis for any marketing campaign. How you decide to run your campaigns depends on the various forms of content. As you certainly would have heard from somebody already, the content is the king. Believe them. Believe them.

Control of the Society

Account management also includes group management. You should be the person to represent brands in social areas and reach out and engage with your audiences continuously. To order to build long-term followers, you must continually improve social relationships.

Public house

Marketing to the same people will not increase your reach and social reach over and over. You should increase the readership and influence of your target audiences.

Service to Customers

Many businesses use social media as a customer service instantaneous platform. You must be attentive and supportive in your social interactions as the first point of touch regularly. You serve the brand and control the views of customers.

Measuring

Any investment effort will have to be measured and analyzed.

Reports

Your customers will want to understand how their investment has been carried out once your efforts are measured and analyzed. This may be visual aids for meetings or digital reports. Reporting is a critical component of any social media manager to demonstrate your value and the added value to the company.

How A Man Became A Social Media Guru?

Since June 2008, he has been active in the social media. This was before all the newest social media resources and applications that are now built into daily social marketers. Reserves or tutorials were not so available that the learning curve could be speeded up.

He found an online course which looked pretty better in teaching him way to turn his social skills into a fully-fledged company on his own account. He invested £ 700 in this online course, and after a few years he will look back and say the value is not all that high, but his ideas. It forced him out of the box to think and inspired him to begin to be a social media boss.

He then attended the University, where he completed his B.Sc. and M.Sc. in Business Management before he wanted to turn his love of social media and network into an independent opportunity. It was then that he jumped into the poker boom and started playing cash games and tournaments online. Poker helped him develop his own skills in time management, money management, and analysis. He always knew he wanted to start his own company so that he could get his feet wet on a secure platform. He has always been involved in online social discussions and even written some guest posts for poker sites throughout his time playing poker.

He was a fully-fledged independent social media manager before he knew it.

In order to promote his freelance social media activities, he has entered a number of networking sites such as Freelancer, ODesk, and Elance. Today, he even uses some of them.

After several years of freelance work in small one-off projects and development of his social marketing skills, he was hired to run his social media campaigns and manage all social marketing campaigns for his own customers by an online business services company. Today he still works with them, showing only the power to forge good working relationships.

In most months of the coming years, he managed to attract customers, and each project was quite different from the next. This allowed him to develop broader skills that he has almost found necessary for a comprehensive social media marketing service. He mentioned some of these more general skills required by the middle of this section to become a great social media manager.

He continued to maintain and construct his own social media profiles. It is essential to practice what you preach and demonstrate your know-how in your own fields. His social profiles have attracted customers regularly who continue to work and build his networking potential.

For a couple of years, he wrote on his blog, but only recently updated his site. He also builds traffic to his websites, where he generates passive income from his own social activities. He likes to "listen" to the social environment and interact with those who already look for its content. This helps to build and strengthen connections and attract targeted traffic.

He was also a frequent blogger member. He believes that the only way to increase your scope and exposure is by writing articles in other relevant blogs. Once or twice, online magazines and publications have published his posts, which are always right.

Keeping his ears on and 'out there' was one thing that he promised to do himself, even if he knew he would spend his vast majority of time in his home office. He tried to meet regularly with business connections and customers to ensure that a real-life person could match online. He even managed to remember his business cards most of the time!

A strategy he's always tried to use while freelancing is to try and turn one customer into three. What he means by word of mouth is the most powerful publicity. People act on strong recommendations made by their friends. He noticed that it was remarkably effective to take the simple method of asking customers at the end of ventures if they knew someone who might profit from social media marketing.

Because social media is such a dynamic environment with startups booming and booming every few months, he knew that keeping social developments up to date was essential. A customer would always ask him to develop profiles or campaigns on sites that some managers of social media have never heard of. Keeping tuned allowed him at least to have some awareness and experience with these channels, which dramatically reduced his learning curve and eventually led to better campaigns.

He expands his services and creates a web design company with his business partner. "Thinking forward" came into being in the summer of 2012. Websites and social media go hand in hand, helping him to up-sell all of his services.

That brings him where he is now loosely. Just to be clear, as a social media manager, he never used paid advertising or SEO for his own sake.

His development was only due to content marketing and guerrilla marketing tactics.

To sum up how he became a master in social media:
- Joined independent pages
- Practiced what he preached and kept his own social media accounts and blogs alive.
- Keep networking and building his contact lists consistently
- Actively develop your own content on your own websites
- Took its content directly to the future
- He kept wondering if people needed his support
- Guest blogging and articles featured
- Networking events attended, and consumer and industry connections met
- Attempted to turn one customer into three
- Maintain up-to-date social networking and development
- Started other initiatives to complement social media services
- Never declined any networking or work opportunities
- Worked long hours to establish integrity, prestige, and presence, often for small rewards.

He thought that he should leave you with some final tips about what he learned from his experiences as a social media boss.
- Sometimes, even if you think you're not right for a project
- If the benefits warrant it, work for less than your desired amount
- You're not going to win all contract, so don't try beat if you turn down
- In social media, things really change quickly, so you have to adapt continuously
- You never know as much as you believe!

It takes time and effort to start a career in anything.

CHAPTER TWO

Identify your target audience

What is your target?

Your company-and every company-has a clear objective: to attract more customers and eventually to own the market.

Today, you do not have to invest more than your competitors in marketing and promoting your company. However, you need a more powerful marketing and promotion engine that generates the full return for every dollar and every hour you spend.

The process of building this motor does not start with strategies but begins by defining your target.

No business-including yours-can afford everyone to market. Of course, it is tempting to try to attract the most significant potential market in the expectation that no prospective customer will fall between your fingers.

However, this approach will actually cost you much more money and bring much less satisfactory results as you have considerably diluted your chances of reaching those who truly serve your needs.

It is important to note that your target market may not include anyone who might ever buy your goods or services. Instead, your target audience consists of those who most likely purchase and thus become the focus of your marketing efforts.

The identification of the right niche is the basis for success in all aspects of marketing and promotion of your business:

It allows you to focus your efforts on those tactics and media, which reach this particular group most effectively.

It helps you to change your sales message to meet the most critical and urgent needs and concerns.

Especially on the market of today, it allows you to build a strong community around your brand of people who love what you do and gladly serve as your fans and evangelists.

And it is the difference between sending thousands and hundreds of thousands of postcards in real dollars and cents to achieve the same end result.

Here are the steps you need to take to make sure you reach the right audience:

Segment your client list.

Who are your clients? Of reality, this question can be answered in several different ways.

Often it is easiest to start by examining your sales data and dividing your customers into groups based on demographic factors such as gender, age, education, income, marital / family status, industry, and location.

When you go through this process, you will usually find that the groups or groups that most often buy from you emerge.

This primary phase will also help you determine whether the same product or service will better be advertised for different groups. Some parts of the market can be more available at trade fairs, while others can be reached home via direct mail.

Dig deeper.

Bridging your consumer base into categories based on essential social characteristics such as gender and income is only step one. You will need a deeper understanding of both their lifestyles and their motivations to reach and interact effectively with these groups.

Start with one of your products or services and evaluate them through the eyes of the customers you have identified within each group. Make a list that includes any reason this customer may wish for this particular product or service. Perhaps they are trying to solve a problem, maybe they just want to feel well with themselves or meet a basic need. This process helps you understand the specific advantages and outcomes that should be at the heart of all your future communication with this group.

Firstly, understand the everyday tasks and how this correspondence is best handled. Should they read the paper frequently? Should you spend a lot of time listening to the radio in the car? Should they turn on the TV or pick up their iPad while looking for news and entertainment? Are they likely to be involved in and, if so, on social media platforms? This form of research is essential to ensure that you choose the best vehicles and media for your attention.

Keep searching.

You have built a strong knowledge base for your target audience at this stage. But if you dig a little deeper, you might find additional details to sharpen your approach.

As you have now segmented your market, and become aware of what drives your customers, see whether you can identify which groups or groups are offering their dollar the most marketing challenge.

For example, which groups represent the most successful of all those who are more likely to purchase your goods or services? In the B2B world, these are usually customers with the most extended service life or those who use the most significant profit margin services.

What are the clients or consumers that give you the most recommendations? These are your best customers because they are selling for you, so make sure you do not only reach your existing customers, but others like them because they represent a group whose needs you serve exceptionally well.

Finally, it would be a weakness not to look at the expectations of the rivals. This is not so that you can simply copy and execute your strategy.

In fact, what you are actually looking for is a market gap that could be overlooked, so that you can slump into and pick up these underserved segments.

Put the test on your goal.

Now that you have identified your audience, it's time for the rubber of your marketing plan, right? Not so quickly.

You have to check your target audience structure to ensure that it supports and grows your business. This process is often referred to as the analysis of SWOTT (Strength, weaknesses, opportunities, threats, and trends).

Tell yourself these questions:
- Can they afford your product?
- Are they going to see a strong need?
- Are there enough people in your audience to support your company?
- How much competition already exists for this group on the market?
- Can you identify any trends you should take advantage of?
- Where will your rates fall in line with your expectations? Too low? Too low? Too high? Too high?
- Does this group have the opportunity to sell other related products or services?

While it may be complex to identify your target audience, these steps keep the keys to competing effectively in today's market if you understand clearly who buys from you and why only then can you find the various channels and become one with your tribe.

TARGET AUDIENCES OF B2B ORGANIZATIONS

Marketing is a strict field of knowledge that is discussed and practiced as a critical ability in the real world in undergraduate classes. The study, design, and execution of marketing methods spend tens of thousands of hours while trillions have already been spent on marketing campaigns by organizations that are trying to make brands very attractive to their target audience. There are still marketing professionals who do not understand the fundamental principles of the practice and end up conducting campaigns that fail to deliver their intended results. This is large because they unwittingly skip some critical steps to the marketing process. These advertisers, in particular, struggle to adequately identify their target audience.

This failure is easy to commit and can be very costly in a B2B environment. Without defining your target audience correctly, you can market your products and services to virtually everyone very quickly. This can be a useful technique, but only in situations with limitless resources. However, as all corporate professionals know, different departments and projects always compete hard for limited organizational resources, making a sparse target audience a feeble basis for designing and implementing a marketing campaign.

For instance, computer graphics manufacturers can easily fall into the trap of showcasing their hardware 's unique benefits in terms of enhancing consumer experiences. This is fine because everybody is fascinated by rich multimedia. In the case of this B2B scenario, the product's net effect on consumers is only a secondary factor. Finally, it is vital that the graphics engineer creates and sets a clear and unique value for computer producers (and perhaps for some big software companies that their products require graphics engines advanced). Because computer manufacturers are chip makers' primary customers.

In some cases, direct marketing to consumers not only waste limited resources but also undermine the effectiveness of the marketing message. When your marketing message is not specifically tailored to the responsiveness of your target market, it will be hard for your audience to understand the value you deliver.

101 Marketing

Let us start by describing what marketing is to bring all these into perspective. The American Marketing Association (AMA) calls it "the activities, set of institutions and processes for the creation, communication, delivery and exchange of products of value for customers, customers, partners and the broader society" and this definition is comprehensive and is worth mentioning for the various stakeholders who are involved continuously in marketing professionals. The first two players are customers and customers, synonymous with the target audience of the practice.

That being said, companies can achieve marketing goals only because they succeed in meeting, anticipating, and satisfying their target audience, particularly in a competitive environment. To ensure that marketing is genuinely successful, all its mechanisms must also take account of the needs and desires of the target audience.

In one sense, critical marketing objectives include creating and differentiating and building differentiated value on the needs of the target audience. Creating and separating means distinguishing your service or product from other similar offers. The more the product or service is distinctive and successful from that of the rivals, the higher the chances of success in the market. Many gurus go so far as to say that a company does not even have to provide the best value for money or conduct the most expensive campaigns but only by having a fundamentally differentiated product that meets the needs or wishes of the target public.

The last clause should give an indication of how to achieve the intended results. It is critical that the target market can differentiate your product from other brands that offer similar advantages. That's not enough, however. Your product differentiation or value should also be that the target audience wants. For instance, you can introduce automotive manufacturers to an efficient and affordable three-wheeled prototype, but if your target B2B client does not or still does not want to embrace the unique value that you offer, your product is really going to be a difficult one. If you have, on the other hand, built an extremely reliable hybrid engine that can be easily found on most vehicles, then there are probably early adopters in your company.

Engage the target group

Many B2B organizations have the challenge of never accurately identifying their target audience. As a result, they are selling to every one of the supply chains, including customers and raw material suppliers. In fact, the vast majority of players in your own ecosystem are really not interested in your product or service. Given that your corporate budget remains small, there is no compelling need to involve them directly, even though you wish to or have a marginal profit. The tactical strategy is to concentrate the attention on the company's most critical players.

If your target audience has yet to be defined, this is a real showstopper. Even then, there is a way around it. Start by identifying the current market your company serves. You can then classify the features or explain the essence of your product or service's target audience. To translate this into a practical context, you can even decide to conduct a social media campaign aimed at making your brand the ideal target audience. Anyway, you need to do this because sticking it with a demographic customer that does not subscribe to or buy your offers is the end for your company.

To help you develop the process further, create a clear picture of what you are offering and the value it brings to your customers. Why do you package your offer? Why will consumers benefit from the purchase of the product or service? You can say, for example, "I sell various kinds of zippers." You can also expand and say, "the zippers can be found in furnace, clothing, baggage industrial equipment, , and sports facilities. Some of our zippers are gravure on marks of consumer products manufacturers."

Now that makes it really interesting to define your product and target audience, isn't it? Please list the key reasons why your customers purchase your product. It may be an inherent product characteristic, such as durability or stylish design. It can be a sales feature like white etiquette that enables your customers to brand the product themselves. You may also offer your company to your customers because of the transactional aspects like volume discounts, low prices, or extensions. Remember that the reasons why your target market purchases your goods tell you all about your goods' problems. Take these into consideration, especially when reworking existing products, new conceptualizing ones, or the strategizing way to market. Regardless of the reasons, list them and weigh their own importance or contribution.

The B2B approach to the target audience

End-users' companies generally use demographics (location, age, revenue bracket, gender, education achievement, etc.) to create useful maps or profiles of their target audiences. Characteristics such as industrial size, credit experience, industry conditions, annual revenue levels, number of employees, and geographical location, on the other hand, are very important components of the client profile for B2B companies.

It is also advisable to consult industry research studies to gain insights into your target audience to help you market your products and services. There are also free reports and web website reports. You can also acquire platforms for social media listening, which generate keywords or phrases often used by industry. This can be used to get a high-level perspective on which needs or issues are discussed more often by different players in your industry and which players are likely to adopt your solutions.

Finally, having an accurate idea of your target audience equips your company to succeed. A well-defined target market can help you to find out whether sufficient potential customers (demand) are there to support your business, configure your offers to meet your customers' expectations, customize or streamline promotions and campaigns in order to deliver optimal returns, and improve cost efficiency by focusing your resources on customer groups. Remember, the target audience would limit only your market, not your company. Instead, it is far better to transmit your message to a small amount of the right listeners than to transfer it to the larger but audience apathetic.

STEPS TO CAPTURE TARGETED AUDIENCE ON FACEBOOK

Major companies spend billions of dollars of resources and only use people to listen to them. But what about small enterprises with no such considerable resources or power to achieve results. You should assume that these MNCs and big business moguls cannot be trusted, but you are incorrect. Even with less capital, you can compete with the big dogs and achieve the best results with more money.

You just need to sit and prepare, which involves all the necessary elements to increase your exposure and stay on top of your game.

The basics are the same, although the way to achieve this goal may be different. Don't worry if you have to go a long way to get there with less money. Concentrate instead on getting there no matter how long it takes.

Stay in service

The best way to ensure that people see you and engage with your content is to make sure you stay engaged. Keep up-to-date with all developments and ensure that you follow them. People are only interested in the materials that are related and unique.

Every day, updating your profile, sharing videos, photos, and quotes are the way to make sure that you are on the market. Using strongly expected hashtags and keywords. Use them in all posts so that whenever some people search for the information, they will find you.

Create a proposal and a sound marketing strategy. Decide your content wisely so that you can stay at the top of your game.

Precious Material

Facebook has modified its algorithm significantly, restricting unwanted posts to followers. This results in the lower organic scope of your website, which affects your analytics directly.

Posts without useful information can not reach the audience, so make sure that you post highly relevant content that will attract the attention of the public. People will be encouraged to share their messages, ensuring virality and wide scope.

This harsh new reality can be done in two main ways: pay each time to promote your most important posts and optimize your unpaid (organic) posts for the best results.

Punctuality

As was said earlier, if the content is not valuable, your organic reach will be reduced. This is just as important now as the people who read the book. What happens when you post original and exciting content, but no one can see it, and all the other ignored materials lose it? You are also making little progress in ensuring your visibility.

For this reason, it is essential to post on specific time slots and schedule posts for prime time. Be sure you understand your target audience, their social media habits, their interests, their routines, so you can post online and actively.

There are several free online tools such as Hootsuite, Buffer, or BleuPage that are able to analyze and provide automation tools for your Facebook page operation. You may use these tools to schedule posts for your target audience and fans at best times. It is vital that you do not post too much, however, to the degree that the flowing posts irritate your followers.

Experimentation

All Facebook pages vary from one organization to the other. Some companies have contents that bring more commitments and interactions such as BuzzFeed, Huffington Post, etc. Some companies, like those who use sanitary products, have less flexibility to post fun content than those previously mentioned.

If you have an average company with less fun content, you have to experiment with all kinds of content. Posts, links, videos, polls, images, memes, etc. are the options to take a shot. This helps you decide which posts are the most appealing to your followers so that you can use the same format for future use.

Experimentation is an essential part of the marketing of social media. Try different posts and compare the reaction of the audience. It also gives you insights that can help optimize new content.

Many software is available on the market and can still be obtained at a much lower price and maximum services. One of this software is the one to use, so here in detail.

PageBlue

BleuPage is a groundbreaking app that enables businesses to advertise products and create mailing lists while subtly and inside their Facebook newsfeed. It provides a two-way conversation with your audience. This lets the company get a broader market that sees the product lead and sell more.

How does it work: You can use the inbuilt creator tool to create a Facebook page. The device is designed to simplify and simplify the process. Once the page has been created, it allows you to customize your posts based on your content. You can drag and drop photos, images, in-forms, diagrams, and much more. Once the material has been posted, users of Facebook can view it immediately or use the "Email Marketing" function to add their email address in the mailing lists box. This lets consumers who are interested in your product and want to learn more about it access future contents directly.

One of the most powerful tools is "Bleupage Gating," which helps your content and posts enter the social media viral world. Once you push a button, your content is viewed by thousands of people. It enables users to view posted information, but not before sharing it with their friends, creating a free traffic stream on posted content.

The program assists you in getting the data, find the best outcomes, and improve your organization to recognize the patterns that attract users.

Research shows that when you read information from others on social media, people spend more than eighty percent of their time viewing their news and timelines (friends, pages, people they follow). This gives the marketing industry the opportunity to promote its products, but since companies' increasing use of social media, an agglomeration of advertising and information attracts public attention. Bleupage is the best communication tool that not only helps you to put your information in the viewing line of the viewer but also stimulates visual content to react to it.

You can schedule your posts, so you don't have to worry about posting or missing all of the information at once.

Targeting Facebook Audience

Public targeting is an integral part of social media marketing, as people play a crucial role in deciding on your business's success and worth. This is why Facebook allows you to choose a variety of factors, such as age, interest, income, education, and hundreds. The process is called the optimization of the audience.

You have to choose the audience you want to reach. Depending on how these people can benefit from your products, you can select one community or a number of different communities.

In order to see which ad targeting options Facebook provides, you can go to the ad creation, pick an objective, and start building your audience.

On the Facebook help page, you can also learn about infographics and type of ad targeting and different audience building options.

HOW TO CONNECT WITH YOUR TARGET AUDIENCES

Until you start planning or carrying out a campaign, it is essential to consider your audiences' expectations and goals and their behavioral trends. It is the only way to connect your non-profit purposes to what's necessary for your viewers (for example, involving advocates to contact state senators on green space protection issues or motivating registration for new parenting education). People can help. People can.

People have traditionally been used to design computer hardware and software, especially website usability. They are being used for publicity and communications strategy, and I believe they have a tremendous interest in the commercial arena:

How can people connect with our target audiences in my organization?

Individuals are potential "stand-ins" of real members in the non-profit. We encourage communications and marketing teams (including authors, managers, designers, and others) to stand in the shoes of their audiences. The communication initiatives focus on supporting the needs and interests of the audience. And you'll find far more success in creating a communication plan or marketing message for a program that meets a particular person's goals rather than trying to plan or write for many people's hazardous needs.

Is Private Another Business Segment Term Just?

No, but that's a growing criticism you may have here from your organization's marketing traditionalists. Market segmentation is a perfect way to define the markets and who you are trying to target. But segmentation of the market cannot shape your marketing messages or choose strategies.

Suppose you are aware that 33% of women 25-40 years old have an interest in supporting breast cancer research and that messages and graphics are critical to their decision-making. Okay, that's a beautiful beginning. Yet people add a lot of money. Somebody may prove that Miriam, 36, wants to get breast cancer today, but she doesn't know enough about how her money will be spent if she gives it to your non-profit. She would like to be assured of how contributions are used.

How can we build people working?

Although people are fictional, they must be strictly and accurately defined. They are ideally based on a sense of a real audience. It is easier to construct accurate individuals if your company is aware of demographics and, better still, of behaviors and interest's data. If you base people on public research, you will make sure that people really represent your audience. Present and future audience interviews are one of the best ways to obtain quality information.

But keep in mind that people can't stand alone. The communications preparation process must be driven by organizational objectives. And it's often essential to test your audiences with messages or multiple versions of letters.

What do you like about a person?

Here's a checklist of sample individuals. The exact details you want to include depend on the marketing and communication goals of your organization. Do you want to increase the use of a new health clinic, motivate volunteers to participate in your mentoring program, or to increase the number of visitors? Regardless of your goals, here's what you want in your people:

- A narrative profile of one to two pages for every user.

- Some fictional information on the life of a person- an interest or a habit which makes every person unique and memorable. When you begin here, the theory builds spring to life.

- A brief outline of day or day at work at home, including specific tastes, details, and dislikes (depending on who you want to reach).

- Name, photograph, age, and personal data.

- Work environments, where professionals instead of individuals are approached, including the duration of work, professional development practices (for example, for marketing services, such as public benefits training for social workers), information-seeking habits and favorite resources, personal and professional objectives, co-workers, etc.

- Technical and personal priorities.

Sample Person-Community Fitness Non-profit Communications Campaign

Context: a non-profit community wellness initiative is initiated and must be supported and inspired by civic politicians, leaders, and residents. The staff must know what is essential for these segments of the public so that they can shape their messages, websites (a central part of the campaign), brochures, and events as appropriate.

Challenge: It is the first time an organization interacts proactively to inspire desirable communities to be created. It will launch a new website, but it does not know how to design the website to educate and motivate diverse audiences more effectively. The coordination team just doesn't know where to begin.

Individual (short version):

John, 65 years' old

John, 65, owns his own home in an industry-based area of Ohio, which is moderately priced. He is married, with two children now living in neighboring countries. John took an early retirement option from the electrical contracting company, where he spent 19 years working. Now he spends most of his free time working in his home and yard and walking around.

One problem John has noticed while walking is that the traffic speed along the road (a connector between two arterial roads) is often well above the speed limit of 25MPH. John told his town council representative, who is, along with John, a member of the local Lions Club, about higher speed. But while the councilman was sympathetic, he did nothing other than suggest that John should complain to somebody in the town or the police. The speeding cars are always going on, and John is feeling insecure as he runs.

Use of the web:

John is a latecomer to technology and the Internet, as many of his age groups do. In recent years, he had to learn to use a computer-based service installed in his truck and tried hard to keep up with the technology that seemed much more comfortable for younger workers in his business.

In order to use e-mail with the children, John purchased a computer but also used many programs like tax prep and QuickBooks software. Its link to Internet is via a single telephone line in the house. It's slow, so John isn't surfing a lot on the Web.

Objectives:

- Slow down the traffic outside his building, through the health of walkers and cyclists.

- Make your district a more pleasant place to live

User:
Once the non-profit met Frank and his colleagues, they were able to form messages and communications that connect with the interests, habits, and objectives of these individuals. They, therefore, knew that they had done their best to maximize the response of the audience.

Readers will try to design or reorganize your marketing and communications service, plan, or product or specific communications campaign today.

Create a Story Brand framework

Marketing efforts must always begin with an agency agreement: a conceptual presumption and framework that catches attention and engages the audience in a way that permeates the mind of each viewer and captures the collective consciousness of the audience. It is the basis of your brand history.

The development of an adequate communication concept is the first step towards creating your own distinguishing marketing strategy: a strategy using the audio-visual performance language to create a brand-related presentation of the campaign. This language of the display includes communication tools necessary to make your product successful and enjoyable.

Technology without knowledge is like a cup of coffee.

The availability of advanced technology at relatively low prices has resulted in a revolution in communication. Every marketing manager and entrepreneur has access to communication options, which have previously only been reserved for major companies with millions of dollars of budgets.

The ability to use easily-learned software and high-tech digital hardware, combined with access to an exponentially increasing internet audience, does not mean that an average businessman has the skills or understanding to communicate effectively within the available internet channels.

I can do it myself, Mommy!

Just as the kid who claims that she needs mom to come to the rescue, the web-media narcissist does need expert marketing communication assistance when he or she wants to survive company-growing pain.

With an e-commerce-catalog and a lot of search engine traffic optimized, your website does not turn into an automated online banker, which takes search engine traffic in one end and spends money on the other. A blog doesn't automatically make someone exciting or exciting, nor does an entrepreneur become a creative director or media star with the possession of a video camera.

Marketing campaigns deal with brands, not products or services, and definitely not features. It's not about the owners, managers, or managers who run things. No, they're about the story, the story of the brand, told in a fashion that resonates and has a meaningful impact on the public.

What we have on the web is a communication venue for everyone, most of whom do not have a necessary understanding of the way to communicate an emblazoned message.

The marketed delivery language

Brands built to the best effect have their own proprietary language, which tells their story, distinguishes them from all brands they compete with, and connects them with their audience in a significant way.

To achieve this sophisticated communication, the language of the presentation must be understood. In a lecture on the four ways sound affects us by outlines the physiological, cognitive, and behavioral impacts of sound on people. The same could be said for performance and visuals for communication elements that create the language of brand presentation together with sound.

If the in-store is valid, it's right on the web as well. Apply to this offensive conversation, graphics and output technologies, and a nightmare for marketing, branding, and sales.

Development of the core concept

Management consultants may encourage managers to build a Mission Statement to function as a strategic roadmap and a framework for tactical decisions, however, unless it is loaded with pointless platitudes and euphemisms that are deliberately designed, it becomes futile and publicly unanimous.

The answer to the problem is, to begin with, what makes you unique. The marketing plan, the high concept behind your organization, and your tactical execution must be based on that aspect of your enterprise that makes you unique, based on specific publicity and promotional initiatives.

The problem is that most businesses do not sell the same products as hundreds, if not thousands of others. It is the company's responsibility to help companies to grow and find innovative ways to achieve their distinctive mark of differentiation. In most cases, the solution is not found in the service, product, or operational procedures but in the manner in which the proposal for emotional and psychological value is presented.

Sustainability of Product Story

What to develop here is a point plan for the future development of a sustainable brand: a methodology that creates a unique brand image rather than a "made-to-service" product, which is outdated with a next price upgrade or a price cut for your competitor.

Up to now, we have four of the cinq elements: a proposal for emotional and psychological value, a contact principle, a distinctive mark, and a language of presentation. Your concept arc is the fifth element. The Concept Arc is how your campaign will lead your audience to where they want to be, and how will you believe them?

In other words, you have access to website traffic, an audience looking for something, the challenge of your brand story is to get into the psychological make-up of the audience and give their audience a jolt of excitement for what it provides. This audience is portrayed by your story scenario and characters, and when your brand representatives move through the traced arc from distrust, skepticism, and approval to desire, so does your audience too.

Your brand history can be built upon various situations: adventure, search, pursuit, escape, rescue, retaliation, performance, underdog status, rivalry, temptation, maturation, transformation, love, self-sacrifice, forbidden fruit, discovery, and struggle.

An Internet Public Can ...

The viewer must be able to understand it with eyes and ears as you see the action unfolding, which needs more than the amount of a number of incidents. Likewise, branding requires more than the sum of characteristics.

The easiest way to introduce a brand strategy, if you have not already found it, is with an ongoing online video campaign, but if you have any questions, consider that an Online audience should be connected to your brand in such a way as to conjure up life experiences, beliefs, attitudes, and precepts. This audience should recognize the characters and discuss their issues, challenges, fears, and needs. This audience must be affected and influenced by sound, visual elements, performance, and mnemonics subconsciously. This audience must be aware of and interpreted on the conscious and subconscious level with verbal and nonverbal messages. And the public must be able to remember and remember the Brand personality so that it becomes a choice of lifestyle rather than a purchase of mere commodities.

All this means connecting with customers on a human level. You may have considerable website traffic or not, but whatever the number of visitors you visit, what is essential is not to allow anyone visiting your site to leave without being aware of what you are doing or knowing why they should look after it.

A strong brand strategy keeps the message alive in different market cycles. The emphasis of the brand message must be on the customer who spends his time or money on you. With a consistent structure in the downward trend in the business cycle, businesses may build protections for brands. In our ever-changing society, presenting your brand image to potential clients or partners is not sufficient, you need to represent your brand throughout your everyday life and spread the message as a story. The goal is to replicate a row. For companies to keep brand marketing in mind, clear and realistic goals must be established.

Companies need to think through incremental blocks in order to achieve realistic goals that give your company a broader perspective of your brand and influential audience. This turnaround allows your brands to grow and change with their demographic target, allowing your business to remain relevant in this changing business culture. There is competition everywhere to have an effective branding campaign, and a bright, unique message must be given to try and counterfeit it will not work.

Branding and marketing campaigns in most industries achieve better returns with videos and images. This is compared with its counterpart to the text base. These trends in society have been common for years because our rapidly evolving community has images that overload our sensory capacity. Video and image campaigns make it possible for companies to submit products to industry-related publications. This enhances visibility by focusing on essential demographics in your industry. Providing work to related platforms is probably the most cost-effective way for multi-level research in your target group. This approach allows you to recognize patterns and sub-categories on the broader population. This will enable you to produce numerous campaign messages, not only to influence the astronomical community, but also the individual.

This approach can show your products and services through amusing media like gallery sites, e-commerce, portfolio websites, etc. If companies submit news related articles on the right platform, once this framework has been developed, it is easy to sustain, but remember that quantity is not quality. If you don't know something, the consumers want to promote quality and innovative experience, not the standard sales pitch. There are only a lot of options, except for the rule!

TIPS TO GET PEOPLE TO TRUST YOUR BRAND

Communicate a strong sense of intent

First, revisit the business intent. The aim should be inspiring for everyone involved in the business. There are very few companies that do not contribute socially. You pick up oil or public utilities, banking, or transportation firms and see the impact on the lives of everyone. The social dimension of an enterprise mission is not a superficial branding aspect. The idea of balance is within this new sense of intent. Shareholders gradually realize that trying to achieve financial results will bite you.

Create a staff committed to your goal

You gain at least two things by articulating your purpose. First, you communicate a consumer advantage (and learn a little more confidence). Secondly, you have more opportunity to achieve this rare thing- employees working together for a common goal. The development of a supportive culture in which workers work together to make a shared goal does not happen incidentally. Collaborative learning involves a coordinated strategy, engagement of staff, the exchange of best practices, and shared policies and processes.

Define "how we do here things."

People want a clear picture of how to behave. These are commonly referred to as values. The fact is that there are many ways to define your business. Shell has its principles of business.

However, there are three key factors:

- Your convictions must come out of your company.

- They must be genuine and strong enough to stay in place when tested.

- And they must be put into practice

The intangible management

Other factors that can add value for your business include a clear strategy, employee abilities, competitive differentiation, a strong board of directors, customer loyalty, reputation, new revenue streams, and innovation. When you manage the values and value of a successful company, you earn confidence.

Build a consistent CSR policy (corporate social responsibility)

In the next decade or so, CSR will merge into corporate governance and corporate reputation. The model Business Impact Task Force and Good Corporation are present, for example, in the UK.

And that varies from company to company. It includes attracting ethical investments, compliance, competitive differentiation, reputation improvement, and winning customer loyalty.

Build a personality brand

Those who gain confidence are transparent, accessible, dedicating and seem to have their individual personality; this is a dynamic personality, you can see in a mood when you step through the reception of Asda HQ in Great Britain. You can see that in the brilliant ideas of Semco from Brazil who turns to 'Max.'

Listen and involve people in odd new ways

When a company is not fingered on the pulse of interested parties' views, it does not have a sense of its company's health. And it is not just good old-fashioned quantitative and qualitative research.

In reality, there are a whole host of new ways to involve consumers, we are already seeing more involvement from digital television, and suggested that companies make use of their market reach to move beyond volunteering workers to social volunteering.

Control risk like confidence risks

New corporate governance standards in the UK and the recent Company Law Review recognize that managers have more specific obligations. They handle risk efficiently and can control chunky financial risks such as more regulations and legislation, Windfall taxes, or customer boycotts.

Institutional transition in power

Businesses still think that ethical corporate responsibility lies in managing the footprint of their social impact, but real progress is made in making use of their muscle for real social change linked to their enterprise. We see a rise in camps that go beyond essential charity or PR to new areas-to work for a single cause and campaigns that make a difference.

It's a hard-balancing act, but it can be done in ways that get trust and offer really social and corporate benefits. There's nothing wrong with the shared gain.

Investment in communications, but the dialog

There are beautifully hidden stories about the commitment of the industry. There are some hidden gems in almost every company, but only the very best don't invest.

- Sometimes they forget that people care about people.

- Perhaps they forget that successful relations are a discussion rather than an annual report.

- And often they forget that we are as involved in future plans as in past performances.

So, what is this? What is this?

So, what're the steps? It's not PR, corporate responsibility, or branding. And what are we debating here? Is it a new idea? Should we call it positive branding or marketing trust? I prefer the common sense of business.

And it's not wishful thinking hair-brained. Today, many of these actions are carried out in companies of many sizes. Also, let's not pretend that only businesses are essential. This applies to governments rather than profits. That's how things go.

Our choice is straightforward. We can create sustainable businesses that are credible, strive for excellent performance, behave wisely, and win confidence, as they deserve them, or we can take a stand against increased customer cynicism. Where would you like to be? In the wake or at the forefront?

READER BASE GROWING SOCIAL MEDIA

You have used most of your time camping on social media platforms such as Twitter, Facebook, and forums if you're anything like the average web user.

While you may like you should invest your time better in your next book, the reality is that it is essential than ever to attract and grow a loyal audience as an author with a strong social media presence.

Social media have become a regular part of life, and if trends over the past two decades indicate that they are here to stay, then we can assume that they will continue to boom as a powerful marketing device.

Will the use of social media lead to further book sales?
Many authors and publishers are afraid to develop and pursue a long-term social media strategy because they believe that it does not help them sell more books.

Although it is true that Social Media is generally not a channel for actively selling books like an e-commerce shopping cart or a dedicated bookselling platform, it can still be used as an opportunity to spread the word on your books widely.

If your message resonates with the right people, it will lead to secure recognition of your brand by word of mouth.

This also builds and intensifies your relationship with communities that are focused on shared values and helps you to provide your prospects with an easy way to know that before the advent of social media wasn't possible.

Social media can only be the tool to get you there faster if you combine it with a full marketing plan.

The use of social media as part of a comprehensive marketing plan will boost your number of people and help you to sell more books, but how?
Social media connect you to the right people in many ways and expand your prospects.

Supports supporting the brand
Brand awareness is one of the most important marketing aspects.
If someone from your target audience sees a marketing message or hears it, and connects it to you and your books instantly, you know that you have a well-known brand.

Generating brand awareness is much easier if you promote your books and yourself through various social media platforms with messages that feature consistent branding elements.

Access to new audiences is easy
One best thing about social media is the convenience with which your existing audience can provide referrals and recommendations.

In a single button, the blogs, photos, photographs, and tweets can be posted quickly to the new people. If they like what
they are seeing or hearing, and it is as easy as another click on a button to support you for future messages.

Increase your website and email list traffic

Social media is a great way to get traffic back to your website.

This is a vital part of a long-term Marketing Plan as it helps you to create an environment in which you can continue to connect with customers, who will only visit your website once and click away and never see it again.

Allows you to gather social data

Consumers are more educated than ever in modern times. Instead of saying that your books are good enough to pay attention, consumers will seek feedback from their peers on your offer prior to purchasing.

It's incredibly important if your books have ever enhanced or changed someone's life enough to share their experiences with others.

Testimonials and reviews are two of the most potent forms of material evidence that can encourage more people to believe in your brand and give attention to it.

Creating and improving partnerships

Another great feature of social media is that you can create and develop a community of loyal fans that will become ambassadors for your brand.

It is incredible how easily they are gathering and taking the initiative to encourage and distribute their message to other like-minded people if you put together enough people under the umbrella of mutual interest.

Enables networking with influencers

Social media has made it simple for almost everybody in the world, including the most influential people in your country.

A fantastic marketing strategy to rapidly increase your readership involves exploiting influencers' audiences.

Think of Oprah, one of the most influential women in the world, and you'll begin really to grasp the power of social media by merely being exposed to others.

Effect on the virus
The Internet viral nature has allowed writers to reach the market rapidly and extensively through sharing peer-to-peer.

This not happen often, but you might find your message spreading like wildfire around the Web if you somehow manage to strike the right chord with your audience.

This allows a large number of new individuals to be introduced within a short period of time.

Pre-selling your opportunities is better
Social media are relevant because they allow you to reach your audience quickly and directly.

Use it effectively and communicate inspiring, educational, and entertaining messages to your reader base outside the book limits.

This can be especially valuable for self-published authors who focus on non-fiction types of writing. Yet social media offers all writers a rare opportunity to highlight the things that make your brand unique and different.

You are continuously pre-selling your audience with snips and previews of what is to come. You bring them closer to buying your books with regular communication and value when they are published.

Over time, you will increase your readers' enthusiasm and passion for your post, your brand, and, ultimately, your books.

Displaying your personality and being honest
Not too long ago, authors were viewed as faceless entities clad behind their publishing companies' iron curtains.

Today, with the introduction of social media and the self-publishing of many authors, this is all changing.

Readers now expect the person behind the manuscript to be known, and social media is the ideal way to do so.

You can let your real personality and voice shine through and make it known to your audience that you are an actual person with feelings and thoughts like themselves.

All these factors lead to a steady increase of your warm-up and ready-to-purchase prospects, which in the final analysis means that you do not promote more than usual through your marketing platforms, but that you produce more reading and selling for your efforts.

Branding More Than Marketing
Imagine you're on a journey of your life. You got pamphlets for a luxury spa. The quarters are luxurious; the grounds are spotless. Images of the signature dishes in the restaurant look delicious.

You 're going to go to the hotel. The room is a mouthful and a little messy. The food is not easy to consume. Service is at best brusque and spotty. You're met with indifference or, worse, silence when you talk to management. You are disappointed and disgusted. With all the sleek ads of the casino, they have fallen terribly short.

Branding goes far deeper than marketing. It will not thrive without ensuring that all facets of your company represent your intended brand and endorse it. You need to be able to express and deliver on your brand one of your most critical assets-your people. This step is especially important for service organizations with no concrete products. They offer soft assets such as information, experience, and men.

If employees don't deliver the label, it can be a death kiss for a company. Conversely, employees who consistently and correctly represent the brand can lead a company to stardom.

Brand: the sum of all its components

Despite what many think, the brand doesn't have your logo, slogan, and brilliant brochure. A good brand combines many essential elements, including organizational strategy, employee contact, customer experiences, and advertisement and marketing activities. As the above story illustrates, your brand extends to your employees, customers, the media, and even the general public. When these components are not regularly improving the brand, consumers would be disappointed if their perception has a negative impact on your business if they express their views to other potential customers or even to the media. This can erode your brand equity and cause misunderstandings about your company on the market, which can lead to prospective employees, customers, and investors passing on your company.

On the other hand, brand consistency at all levels helps an organization to grow and prosper. Strong brands can drive sales growth. The business is ideally known for recruiting and keeping the best employees. Sellers will see your brand's value and pursue partnerships with your business, while investors know the company and your brand equity as a valuable asset.

Branding by the workers

Your staff is one of your customers' most critical points of contact. Here are several steps to ensure that your brand is represented in the best possible light.

Develop the philosophy of an organization. The first step to improve the brand among your employees is a thoughtfully designed strategy that governs how your business operates.

Maintain consistency of the brand. This is a crucial step to build a strong brand. It is also one of the first moves to unravel, however. All aspects of your organization need to be consistent. But it is not enough to set expectations. You have to analyze your actions continually. Set control points for any part of the organization that communicates with consumers and the general public. Make sure every employee is empowered to recognize and address inconsistencies in your brand. If a customer fails to deliver on a brand, he or she could forget. Otherwise, and he or she might not be so forgiving. It takes only a few to dissipate the brand you are branding.

Practice what you say. Examples are the best way to lead. If your brand plans to support your organization and then abuses that promise, your brand (and sales) will suffer. Point of the case: Wal-Mart. The company says: "We believe that our people and how we treat them are one of the keys to our success." The store chain has, however, been unjust salaried wage lawsuits. Furthermore, although they say they value their target customer (the hard-working middle class), their actions are not necessarily rhetorical.

Deploy brand guidelines. Your organization must create a framework or set of brand guidelines for all to follow to ensure brand consistency. We 're not only talking about the logo or corporate identity guidelines, and we 're talking about brand specifications, brand identity guidelines, key messages, core values, brand attributes, measurements of success, and processes for dealing with customer issues or feedback. An Internet-based software detailing the company's brand instructions is used by international shipper. This comprehensive approach offers guidance on all facets of the company logo's graphic standards to how the brand's cultural difference affects (particularly important for global businesses). Establishing brand guidelines leaves no room for misunderstanding and ensures that all levels of the organization are consistent.

Cultural gaps in comprehension and discussion. We are really becoming a global economy with advances in technology, communications, and the Internet. It is more important than ever to consider cultural differences when developing a brand, especially when your company has an international reach. Words and phrases in America in another country may not translate into the same meaning. In the United States, what customers value and perceive as positive is radically different elsewhere. In the past, the US was the model that everyone else wanted to follow. Today, this is not necessarily the case. It is, therefore, up to companies to ensure that their brands transcend such cultural differences if their geographic reach is to be more significant.

The brand goes far beyond your marketing efforts. Your brand is just as good as the people behind it and the people before your client. Take the time to build a corporate culture that reflects your brand adequately. Train your staff to represent the brand. Assess the quality of your brand in all aspects of your business. You will strengthen your brand equity and make your company more successful.

CHAPTER THREE

Mastering social marketing spectrum

Social networking has become the buzz of the world of Internet marketing. At first, it was a vague approach to visiting a new class of websites and trying to get your company or website involved. These networks are known collectively as the world of web 2.0 or social media websites. We now know that you will find one of the keys to creating traffic through these new channels on your website.

A social networking website is any today's service, website, or tool which makes use of community interactions, which allows users to create their own content, share it with others, and connect with other users. This range includes many of the world's most popular websites, from

Facebook to Twitter and YouTube. So how can they be used to generate traffic successfully for your online company?

The problem for most people is that they expect to be able to log in, create an Account, and wait for a viral traffic storm at their doorstep the next day. Although social networking can be easy to generate traffic, it's not that simple, and you must make more effort to succeed.

The first rule is that you will not be able to expect one of these services to be an outlet for your ads or press releases. You can't just walk out there, spillover, and expect results from your service. What you need to do is become a faithful group member-is can't make it just about social networking? You must take part in conversations regularly, respond to tweets, support what other people say, add people to your friend's list, set up and join groups, and more.

If you do all this, you create a real presence for yourself that can lead to traffic that you have never seen before. You will be a genuinely respected voice in your community, and people who feel the same about the same issues will follow you and will finally check on your website. Even if you don't express strong opinions, you can still reach others by just getting out and making yourself known to as many other people as possible.

Social networking involves all using the web to connect and share your own voice with other people. For numerous reasons, businesses have been keen to use this massive force, including to generate traffic back to their websites. Many have failed because they simply don't understand the fundamental things that you really need to get involved. You will succeed in social networking if you can master this concept and actively engage your community.

Social media marketing has a falsified reputation. To several executives in the marketing team, this is a sporadic and, from time to time, postings, interactive, and ads over Facebook and Twitter to a set in registrations through many social networks. This certainly isn't the right shot!

SMM is not only present in the field of social media. It is a robust commercial commitment that can only become complete havoc if not properly handled. The objective of social branding in cyberspace is like the real world. It is about supplying single selling points to concrete and sustainable sales. It's about at best turning an anon into a brand defender. Attaining this goal necessarily follows exactly the same rules except that social media allows a closer, more customized, and flexible approach to the goals, to put it another way. But with more or fewer variations, the same rules apply. Evaluation of prerogatives, environment, context, and tools is a crucial basis for any social media marketing campaign. It implies careful configuration and clinical accuracy in how messages and attitudes are supplied via dedicated channels. Posting on Facebook, group page, a fan page, or personal page is not the same process in such campaigns.

Once you launch Social Media Advertising, here are checklist points:

Defining your grassroots strategy. Create a roadmap budgeted with the intermediate white stones which will help to fine-tune the campaign throughout. The roadmap must remain in keeping with what is being done or done in the real world. Marketing in social media is rarely an innocent act. It takes time and will incur costs. To be accurate about the campaign will undoubtedly reduce the burden. As mentioned earlier, evaluate the main goal and methodology. You can need to fully update your actual website, for example, to allow SM and SMO integration. Make your campaign Measurable, SMART-Specific, Relevant, Realistic, and Timely. Go for conscientiousness or sales or loyalty. One by one! One by one! Don't try in one go-to aim for all goals. Remember! Remember! Stick to the marketing and communication policy of your company.

Assess and understand the environment of your campaign. RESEARCH, and don't stop till you get sufficient! Without necessary precautions and headlamps, one certainly would not like to jump into the dark waters. So, with your campaign for social media marketing. TOTAL MESS can be especially important when it comes to building awareness and product reputation. To develop a successful online media strategy needs to understand fully what rivals do on shared channels (of course), but above all, take a modest glimpse of how other people from various sectors do or do. Get into positive case studies as well as failures. Learn about the technical capabilities of all social networks and platforms.

Identify these platforms and instruments that are relevant to your roadmap and that respond positively. Social media marketing aims to send the same consistent message across the entire spectrum of interwoven social networks. The winning triumvirate consists of Facebook, Blog, and Twitter, to which you can add a YouTube account if the video clips are uploaded regularly.

Budget and size your online ads realistically. Using Google AdSense and Facebook advertisement platforms to their full potential, but be careful to aim wisely. Marketing campaigns for goals mean nothing without proper advertising. Intuitive online advertisement is now accessible by a few clicks and undoubtedly unleashes the ability to communicate on a global level about your brand. We can also increase the spread to small areas. Consider identifying and evaluating your geographical targets. This helps to maximize the budget for online ads. The choice of PPC or CPC corresponds to your fundamental roadmap requirements.

Set up a taskforce for social media from the team and search for an outside person to serve as a group manager. The web never falls asleep. Social media marketing is a continuous roll-in 24/7. As such, time and resources are needed. One cannot expect to be able to handle a social media marketing campaign alone, mainly if other primary duties of the organization are involved. Instead, invite some of your staff to participate in social networking on behalf of your business. But be chosen! Those who undertake such a sensitive and interactive task should write well, be creative, touching, and loyal. International community managers are rarely inclined and are solely responsible for the consolidation of the activities of your taskforce through the relevant social networks. In any event, you should establish a team whose main goals and skills are learning, listening, and responding tactfully.

Get your team to recognize critical bloggers and social media activists who border your areas of interest and industry. This mission is one of the hinges of your campaign success. Speaking of heavyweights in social media is like recruiting evangelists when partnerships are established. Having Lady Gaga like your boots is like tipping into a sea of opportunities as broad as nine million people who will follow Gaga's recommendations. If she purchased one, it would mean instant success. However, Alert! The adverse effect is often proportionally as high as the reputation of your touch. Make sure you're selling to him or her. Here is a successful social media marketing strategy.

Identify relevant instruments for measurement and benchmarking. These are indicative of the success of the campaign or the need for fine-tuning. For example, an increase in the number of people on Facebook or Twitter followers is an indicator of the health of your campaign. Learn how often your brand is mentioned on the web and evaluate these comments to help to get the campaign right. You should also be able to monitor your growing relationships and traffic from social platforms. Identifying future prospects helps to develop better strategies. Be careful! Social media metrics can be tricky in the current state of affairs! You will actually need an extensive range of results combined with trend reports to show your campaign's accurate snapshot.

Identify offline components to complement social media marketing. Offline events are essential tools for conversion in the correct and appropriate manner. Offline components may also mean socializing, giving real-world prizes and donations, bar parties, holding meetings, workshops, and conferences, with people of the site, etc., Determine how these components can improve the brand experience of your goal and how they fit into your online marketing scheme.

For the posting of posts, multimedia and comments, request quality-related information. The perfect tactic to applaud your 270hp 1974 Red Corvette as you promote green goods on your blog. Make sure you lay editorial rules that define the consistent production of cross-platform content in terms of both readable literature and technical details. Can a video be posted on HD on YouTube and Facebook? How much time should an article last? Does an essay have a specific generic line for many writers, or should it carry the name of the author, and for what reasons? These lines should always be defined according to the target audience.

Call for HUMAN to stay at every stage! The social media marketing strategy is to build a social media presence of your brand where your available quality content delivers your organization's values. Social media is, First of all, socializing! People are touchy with behaviors and behavior; they don't like bullying or being viewed as childish customers. The social experience is too techy, too commercial. The basics of the best approaches are simple language and "real-world" politeness. It is sometimes more fruitful to begin a discussion far away from your product and your campaign goals. High conversion rates are never far ahead with a willingness to listen and the power to communicate clearly.

Anyone who participates in social media marketing would have to rely on a vast number of strings at the same time. It is essential to understand the climate of the campaign through research and pre-dive learning. Although the marketing process may look like the world of reality, the online social experience means that you master every stage even more precisely, because you can never see or analyze real-time behaviors, apart from what is written from behind the monitor, if correct or wrong. A Social Media Marketing Strategy is simply the result of a combination of individual skills and web tools that enable a brand's social interaction and exchange. The seller has an obligation to be a sociologist, psychologist, or ethnologist on-site in two-way traffic. You don't necessarily have to do so because you are a human being who is allegedly used to modern psychological codes.

SOCIAL MEDIA EFFECTIVE ENGAGEMENT

The last holiday season was possibly the most considerable publicity in Lebanon and the Middle East of the year. Many brands hope to improve their social media marketing efforts to use the many opportunities they offer and to avoid significant marketing falls. As ad space becomes scarce, more brands look to take part, despite the fact that publicity costs skyrocket and opportunities to make an impressive fall.

In Lebanon, as well as the rest of the region, digital literacy has become an increasingly common source of entertainment, research, and socialization, particularly during Ramadan, where people have significant free time.

But how do you achieve higher quality advertising and hit your social media target audience at an affordable price?

Know the client

Usually, this is the starting point for each marketing plan. Businesses claiming that they know their target market exclusively by practice often squander vast sums of marketing money and end up being fooled by their ROI.

We always find it useful to define the target consumer of the customer and then to back it up with sound research. When you do not know how to identify a target audience, it can be beneficial to design people. People are imaginary, common representations of your ideal customers. You can personalize a portion of the market you are trying to attract.

Using research, CRM, the feedback of the sales team, social media interactions, and your own experience, it might be helpful to build people on:
- Age.
- Rental.
- Preferences and Comportments.
- Revenue.
- Social networks on which they are most involved.

You might want to create several buyer people, each representing a single segment if you have several target audiences. Then you can allocate as many demographic and psychographic data as you think fit.

This can be a lot of fun, particularly if your graphic designer wants to play them in a popular television show like funny cartoons or characters.

One hidden advantage is that you could explore new audiences you never imagined before. You can hire an intern or host a group with teenagers from your family if your individual is a teenager, and you do not know what teenagers have done since N'Sync was popular.

You may find it harder to address the psychographic angle of your personality because there is so much information that is important to how and why people make their buying choices. Maybe you want to ask yourself:
- What is their favorite contact method? Telephone or e-mail?
- What motivates them to use social media?
- How much are new items being tried? How relevant is peer assessment?
- What are the expectations of them? That's a brilliant issue. Higher motives for customers often influence the type of content you share (message, voice tone, picture, etc.).

Research shows that in Ramadan, consumers around the Arab world tend to watch more videos, search more, and spend more time on mobile devices.

As every experienced marketer says, seasonality is significant.

The same study shows huge jumps in search during Ramadan for any other Gulf country. Then the volume of the search period drops back to a flat line after Ramadan, reflecting the return of the beverage to relative online obscurity.

Your market knows

Once you have a good feel for your audience and how it works online, you can estimate the size of your public with Facebook Ads Manager.

Google Analytics also provides an environment where visitors can understand how they communicate with your website: where they come from, how they come, and what services they want. These insights can help you to reduce social media advertising costs. In Google Analytics, you can see which networks your audience works with you under the Acquisition Tab. Visiting Facebook Insights to validate your findings is a good idea.

Now, let's take a look at your rivals. Facebook is the epicenter of social networks and is, therefore, the best way to start and see how active your competitors are. Go to Facebook Insights and click on 'Add Pages' in the 'Overview' button. Choose three to five competitors.

This step enables you to keep an eye on the activities of your competitors and tell you how their audience engages on Facebook.

Follow your Instagram and Twitter competitors too. Figure out what hashtags they use and how many times they upload or tweet images. Any competitor you can think of on an Excel sheet is a good idea to write before adding their Instagram usernames, and Twitter handles in neighboring columns.
Another smart idea is to build a Twitter competition list. Don't hesitate to privately make it.

Facebook provides many tools for reaching your target audience. Did you use the device Audience Insights? You can gain many valuable insights into your audience using audience insights, for example:
- Likes page
- The population
- Use of Facebook
- Site and Language

Another great way to extend your Facebook audience is to target audiences with a look. You select a source audience when creating a Lookalike audience (a customer service established with a data partner, pixel data, mobile device data, or page fans). The characteristic qualities of the people on Facebook are then identified (e.g., demographic information or interests).

Now that you have identified your audience, how exactly do you grow and maintain social media customers? I believe that the answer lies in two key elements:

- Content type is released on these platforms
- Nature of the platform for social media users and

Let's take Facebook. Let's take Facebook. Facebook closes on the milestone of 2 billion. The first quarter saw 80 million new users making a considerable contribution to 1.94 billion active users monthly and 1.28 billion active users daily.

But is YOUR Facebook audience? If yes, remember the following guidelines that have worked for many of my customers:

- Post regularly, if possible daily
- Repost original material but never adopt the same style or text. This is especially important if new content is challenging to come up with. Experiment with images, videos, or infographics. For Photoshop and Canva, WordSwag, you can use Ripl and iMovie for videos.
- Seek to plan for your posts to be the most successful for your audience.
- If you plan to repost, use a new title.
- Improve your exposure by requiring the members of your team to share the original and its modifications on their accounts.

The Ad Success Test

Run your analysis now that you have defined your audience and have experimented with content and publication. Facebook offers the Ads Manager a great analytical tool. You can measure the performance of each ad against its audience. You won't be able to assess which social media strategy is working well without analytics. When a promotion is less than anticipated, compare it to other announcements, research the cost per result, and try to figure out what is wrong. It may be the voice tone, message, picture, or something else. It is safer to focus on two platforms that perform well than on any social media channel.

Finally, inject your brand with some personality. To those of you unfamiliar with the brand, it is a restaurant on Facebook and Instagram with an excellent presence. They never fail to disappoint their customers with active discussions, funny pictures, and almost always exciting content!

Decide on your brand identity and focus on content that reflects that identity. Add exciting content to the mix and follow a proven brand.

Lebanon 's people are becoming more online than ever before. This trend is only increasing in the Holy Month. If your audience is defined correctly, and a high content strategy is chosen, there is plenty of opportunities to reach and form your target audiences' perceptions.

What is Search Engine Managed Marketing?

Managed SEMs can be benefited virtually by any website owner. Search engine marketing usually focuses on positive ROI (return on investment) with its broad spectrum of popular internet marketing resources, predominantly search engine-based resources. In other words, the idea is to use it with your site to make money.

What is search engine marketing done precisely?

Well, for beginners, it is traditional SEMs, which include organic SEO, pay per click ads (PPC), and other search-based marketing technologies. The overall strategy sometimes includes social media and other non-search engines based on online marketing techniques.

The concept is to use organic search optimization to build an automatic and lasting basis of targeted inbound traffic from the search engines. This is the SEO portion of the program. In addition, pay per click internet advertising is used, and expertly implemented to deliver conversion results from day one for almost instant targeted traffic.

Pay per click advertising is sometimes regarded as too expensive, but when professionally implemented to achieve results-oriented objectives, it should generate a positive ROI right from the start. So it costs a certain amount to purchase the advertisement and pay for the clicks, but the increased revenue or the outcome will pay more than the cost per click.

It is complicated to develop an overall SEM strategy. Many website owners tried to do both SEO and PPC themselves ... often with stellar results. And it can be dissuasive.

Here comes the "management" part of managed search engine marketing.

Why would experts not invest a lot of time, energy, and financial resources on trialing and error in developing an efficient SEM plan? Fully managed SEM outside your web marketing is truly the best way to make the most of your online marketing in the game early. Managed search engine marketing is generally carried out at a fixed rate, ensuring that marketing costs are consistent and achievable (and the results are noticed much sooner).

Scaling up your digital business

Small business owners take advantage of postage scales now for one day. A postage scale weighs your mail and letters to give you an accurate understanding of the cost of the post. When the USPS postage price increases, you just want to adjust the postage meter accordingly. Usually, this is done by a microchip. You would just acquire another microchip and then adjust your scale accordingly if you need to keep your scale informed for the exact post.

Some scales will give you an assessment rate for other services like DHL, Fed-Ex, and UPS. This is a significant advantage that enables your trade to save even more money by saving money cost-effectively.

Shipping Supply Posting Indicator

The postage indicator differs from the postal scale because your symbol is the element that actually stamps your mail. Basically, a postal range gives you a load. Under federal legislation, the USPS can't sell a postal indicator - they can only allow you to sell one.

Your display indicator will set you on your shipping supplies enormously. You can not only take care of the leading shipping projects from relieving your home office but also professionally stamp all your mail with "metric" marks.

If you spend more than $50 per month in shipping, then it is most likely that you will benefit from a leased postal indicator. Your postal display will hold up to $1,000 postage value at a time. If you need more postage arrangements, you can attach your telephone line to your indicator and download more postage from your USPS store. This saves time in the fact that every time you want to mail a business letter or package, you won't have to run off the shop.

Scales for Digital Posting and Shipping

You can also buy digital shipping scales that suit UPS well. These scales are useful for sending as well as receiving. A UPS postage is perfect for mailrooms and office mail management. Again, make sure your chosen size of preference will comply with the weight restrictions you need, as well as the appearance you need.

Some features to manipulate your selection of UPS scale include easy digital readings, ability to attach your UPS scale to a computer, accurate readings, protecting shocks and surplus, the ability to handle gross weight measurements, and rechargeable batteries.

When using UPS appropriate scales, you can quickly be assured that your company will be able to cope with all the mailroom needs, shipping, and packaging requirements and manage storage weights.

Industrial scales find their rightful place in the business sector by far. These weighing instruments are considered the most appropriate solution for weight calculations, for all your industrial needs, for accurate, well-balanced weighting solutions, and more. The marketing of these scales, however, has dramatically affected the overall operation of companies.

In general, you can choose the right weighing scale for your business with a wide range of options. Some of the most commonly used are listed below.

- Enforcement
- Crane.
- Space for the bench
- Pallet
- Floor
- Shipping
- Internet and more.

All the scales above can be used for various purposes in industries, such as the agricultural industry, pharmaceutical industry, transport, medical industry, food industry, petrochemical industry, etc. These dimensions are also classified by size, capacity, design, price, and style, so the right choice is better, with a view to achieving high efficiency and avoiding unnecessary trouble, including a waste of time and money.

Below are some points that you may think of in order to purchase the one that meets in the first place all your industrial requirements.

i) Identify your company needs – it is essential that you first determine all your business needs, including loading and costs factors. After you have done this, you can quickly move to the next phase, i.e., compare various options.

ii) Evaluate various options-look for various options available on the market these days and choose the one that meets all your identified requirements. You may even submit estimates, explore limitless possibilities, and also compare prices with your various choices.

iii) Demo request-the, the option of a suitable industrial scale, is undoubtedly an inertial activity to perform; therefore, it is critical that you request a demonstration if you go for an industrial scale. Moreover, many dealers give their customers a free sample, so that it is easier to approach them first and then think about buying the one according to your needs.

iv) Proper consultation – regardless of what your requirements are, you should consult someone with immense knowledge in this area, or you might even research a little before you begin with the next BIG task, i.e., purchase the right scale for your business.

It is undoubtedly quite a problem to select the right industrial scale for your trade, so it is essential that you consider the above-mentioned points to ensure that the process is hassle-free!

DIGITAL MARKETING METHODS

The digital services breakthrough opened the door with a wide array of ways to sell your product. It's become a science itself to develop your digital marketing strategy. For years we have been targeted, but most people don't know that they are online.

Yet what facilities do your business currently have?

Online advertisements

Digital advertising on websites has become a smart way of selling your message. Services like Google AdWords have the ability to get your news to the people you 're looking for. Say, you 're selling remote control cars, so your ad on a holiday website won't boost sales. You have to maximize your advertising budget and use a targeted system to reach the right demographic and take into consideration the views.

Although this market is highly competitive and only targets those who already visit sites that are related to your company, breaking new customers who do not know your industry is challenging.

Search Engines Optimization

The way to reach new people is to make your website search engine friendly. If a new user has a question or tries to find the information, they use a search engine. Making your search engine friendly is an ever-changing field with Google and Microsoft using state-of-the-art search algorithms to analyze Websites. Now, you need at least daily updates to keep your website up to date and well placed within the search engine results.

Search engines are not just making their judgments on the site you have and the information you have provided these days. This needs to be validated for creating a backlink database with details on other websites. When knowledge increases, search engines must have this legitimacy to avoid the creation of search hijacks and misinformation presented to the user in their results.

The market is a very critical aspect of a marketing strategy, with the traffic of search engines usually responsible for more than half of all visits to a site, which cannot be ignored.

Social Markets

Social marketing is a new sector but has the potential to achieve excellent results. Social networks bring many people together to connect with each other in one way. You can post your opinions, views, maintain touch, create friendships, develop online communities with common interests, and "chat" each other.

This large amount of data is a dream come true for marketing. The days are gone when you wanted endless hours of market analysis and study. You can view interests and topics that change at an hourly rate in real-time. You can target critical trends with your message and receive feedback over long studies and feedback that are required with traditional marketing methods in a short time. Advertisements that are used in household systems and user groups can aid socially structured products but are wasteful on everyday products and consumables. Washing powder firms can't use this kind of advertising channels because their advertisements won't be taken seriously and are best used for more traditional services such as in-store advertisements and coupons.

There are some rule exceptions with the return of the Wispa bar Cadbury had a good campaign, set up by a small group of people and re-established the bar and provided the brand a significant boost in the national media. The campaign was successfully launched by using social networks to build online follow-up using website users to promote the cause with the brand's popularity and nostalgia. Cadbury then decided to listen to the number of consumers and replicated the product in limited quantities, sold it out in record time, and then re-implemented it in their current line as a permanent commodity. The people of the campaign were thought to be a small marketing team who used the broad scope of Facebook and Twitter to "snowball" the drive to succeed.

Social networking should not be pushed aside. If the campaign is smart and supported continually, it can really help your business as it is now easily lost in the mounds of information produced by networks like Twitter and Facebook.

Campaigns Viral

The advent of social networks and the growing use of video and other media platforms have driven the online campaign to a new dimension that has merged an off-line initiative with technology brands as well as entertainment.

Companies like Microsoft have used this to a large extent with the Xbox 360 announcement. The users had to follow a six-month-long crumb bread trail before the decision was made at E3 in 2005. They used the reach of online communities, put real-world physical clues, "hidden" messages on coded Websites. They generally contributed to another hint that the devoted army of users wanted to find the news first to decipher. For their benefit, media organizations have looked for this and did not give them time to the leaks and intimate knowledge they usually have in this sort of application.

The entertainment industry now always uses this type, but not as significant as before. They are now usually sniffed out and lose credibility because new campaigns have no effect whatsoever.

Marketing Email

Spam is one of the oldest terms in the technology industry and has been accepted by many cultures in general. It refers to a sketch for Monty Python, a favorite of early programmers who used it as a guide for unwanted material sent to them via the electronic mail system.

E-mail marketing has now lost much of its credibility. An average of 183 billion spam emails are sent per day, so the virtual post will lose your advertisement account. Spam email systems are ingenious, and they use sophisticated algorithms to evaluate the contents and origin of the email and to determine whether or not they spam. They usually block all ads, as spam emails can maliciously trick users into providing personally identifiable data or spreading computer viruses to a large scale.

Studies have shown that spam emails cost businesses more than $200 trillion a year to legal systems and governments worldwide. With the introduction of more and more complex ISP-level systems, it is becoming challenging to use email as a viable means of sales. During the 'now' it was the king of advertisements as more and more people use it as a reliable communications system, now it's a shadow of its old self.

Over the next few weeks, we will study the systems further, determine which combinations you should use, how you can use them, and the best methods for obtaining your information in the best possible way.

DIGITAL BUSINESS MANAGEMENT

It is accurate and precise that today's organization, from what we know as analog, really grew into the new technological business. There we will discuss the transition of global trade from analog to digital, the post-digital age of industry, the problems faced by various companies in the pre-digital period, the benefits of the numeric business period, and why this company needs to be digitalizing over the internet (if not yet done) for a secure and accurate solution.

The Pre-Digital Management Business Era

During that period, which we could call the dark ages in business, so many companies only rotated in one place, without much branch and extension. Industries, even when quality service delivery, effective business communications, and contact outside the territory, are ineffective, where it is located like what we are all about today. In the Western world, as we refer to it, this period ended faster than we began compared to what we had during the digital business revolution in so many countries.

Precisely, this analogous business method remained (in the midst of global digital business awareness on the Internet even) until at the beginning of the 21st century (that was when the country embraced democracy in its third republic), when most companies, mainly banks, started digitizing their businesses, after seeing the quality of service they could provide.

Market organizations and customers for pre-digital business age.

If I may ask you or like anyone else, are there challenges that companies have faced throughout that pre-digital current business world? The humble reply is yes. Many customers (e.g., for banks and other businesses), clients (for private companies), and even the employees of these aforementioned companies were confronted with.

In banks, some customers have complained about how long it takes to move some money in another retirement branch, in fact, even before this time because you can't just make payment in an office and withdraw it in another. But it's all in the same branch where both deposit and withdrawal are made. This was the blight of so many bankers, and the advantage of highway robbers since the individuals who do an interstate business must all travel with their raw cash.

There have been many victims of this highway robbery, while some have even caused the deaths of the persons involved due to un-digital businesses in the banking sector. The work was rather dull to some workers in most banks during that time, as they would need to move files from one desk to another that would hold one or two functions. This has resulted in many graduates fleeing banking jobs because of the challenges of the job before.

Today, however, the story is certainly different. Even graduates clamor for the job, but very few. Banks were not the only institution to experience such challenges during this time, such as private companies, public liability companies, conglomerates, federal government-owned institutions such as customs, immigration, to name just a few. We learn in immigration that it took much longer for an applicant to receive an international passport application than it is currently possible to obtain.

Organizations and benefits digital and post-digital business.

When work for banks and others becomes tedious and incredibly demanding, the hunt for a better way out and an efficient market expansion has begun to take place. These led researchers to seek a way to bail out this search and also make money for themselves. So many programmers began to write computer programmers, computer networking began, organizations started using computers to maintain records as well as international (internet) networks became the order of the day.

Federal government institutions, both private and public, now have their worldwide web (www) and domain name. Video cameras now used for proper documentation to keep events. GSM companies have saved so many local telecommunications firms who have had the revolt before us. Today, you can manage your company easily without having to fly by phone and email (e-mail).

As we said before, most of us took digital business not until the end of the 20th and beginning of the 21st century, and as we did, we were glad that we had done so. Today, business is free, stress reduced, business growth is increased, profit is reduced within a short time. We can see on the Internet today globally the impact or rather the advantages of the post-digital business period. The Internet is now the worldwide center of business villages in which people meet their needs.

Research can be done online, and people can make trustworthy friends online and even meet their soul mate and another online business host.

People can also trade foreign currency (forex) in the comfort of their offices and in Closest today and profit enormously without having to travel or know the broker, thanks to the digital business or electronics business.

For businesses that are yet to take advantage of this time saving and trustworthy business model, in a world, you have to stand up and do it regardless of what it takes to pay more. As we said in our introduction earlier, it will give you an accurate, reliable, full, timely, and accurate result.

Digital business strategy has proven to be today's most convenient and accurate business method. You could save the costs of physical recruitment of your entire organization and recruit online and then see that it has been proven to be a time- and resource-saving exercise. After reading these comments, we hope that you think of going digital every time you think of business because it will help you to achieve it a lot earlier, just as you anticipated.

CHAPTER FOUR

Generate solid profit incomes

Will you decide to become a marketer affiliate?

You must first choose which products or services you are promoting assumes you have been searching for and finding a competitive market, and a promotional strategy is in place to start making money. You now have to choose services, products, programs, and traders that fit your overall niche and marketing plan.

This can be very difficult to select partner services. It can be a painful trial and error process for many beginners for a while. But if you decide on good affiliate programs, you do not need to apply these key points.

1. Which Commission are you going to be paid for? This is usually the first thing new affiliates are looking at because they would like to know how much money they can make for each sale. And most people choose to promote products that offer very high fees. What they don't know is that sometimes with lower commissions you can make a lot more money.

It's not really the rate of commission. That's the most important thing. It's the amount you're going to be billed for. If you choose to promote a $25 product or service just because you're going to earn 75 percent of the sale, every time you sell, you're only going to get $18.75. While that might look good, better options could be available. Suppose another product is trading at $100, but only 30% of commissions are available.

Would you just pass it because fees for the percentage appear lower? Sadly, many would and often would. But you will realize something in the examination: 40 percent of a $200 sale is $40. Almost twice what you can produce with a commissioned product of 75 percent. Don't even make the mistake of choosing goods or services based solely on the sum of the fee. Think of the real dollars you can make with a healthy affiliate plan instead.

2. The next critical element to consider is the conversion ratio. How many of those visitors will actually take out their credit card and buy if you send 100 targeted visitors to a corporate sales page? The percentages matter a lot in this situation. If 1 % of people buy, it is a 1% conversion ratio, which means that an average of 1 out of 100 people will buy. But if a commodity has a conversion ratio of 10 percent, then ten people out of 100 can buy. If you combine conversion ratios and commission rates, you can learn more about which product you can promote best.

Let's assume the 75% commission product has a 2% conversion ratio, and the 40% has a 4% conversion ratio. As you already know that the 30% product makes more real dollars, it's no brainer to stick with it because it has a higher conversion rate as well. However, if the 75 percent product has a 10 percent conversion and the 40% conversion figure is marginally more senior, you'll probably change your mind. Because no matter how much money a product can earn, if people don't buy it, it'll not be profitable.

3. Let's take a look at the Sales Page now. Many new affiliate marketers are missing this move. Visiting the sales page on which you send prospects and seeing Google AdSense on that website, maybe it's not a smart idea to promote it. Why? Why? If you are posting visitors to the page and they don't buy them, they will click on AdSense advertising from the merchant and make money from the merchant when leaving you.

The same applies if you have other affiliate links on your list. If you've signed up for another affiliate program and put those affiliate links on the page from which you are trying to sell, it might make other affiliate sales from the links, but you would not earn any money again. Sometimes another problem may arise with traders selling physical products. It is not difficult to find a telephone number free of charge on the sales pages.

The trader needs a number in order to ensure that the sales are not lost, but if they are very prominent, the potential customer that you have sent to the website will simply collect the phone and bypass you. However, some traders handle this problem well and put a referral code next to their phone number. When the future customer calls, he asks for the system to track you, so that you can receive sales commissions.

4. What are the words of the merchant? This is another crucial thing most new affiliate don't know they need to examine carefully. Many retailers put sly exemption clauses in their contract terms, and members do not see that they will not be charged for different sales. Some people may say, for example, that affiliates won't earn commissions on phone orders.

Others may say that affiliates can only earn commissions, but not others, on certain items. Some trading terms stating that the member can only sell once, ever. So, if the customer bought something every day, the first thing they purchased would only be paid for. In this case, you must be alert and stay away from such programs.

5. What are the terms of payment? You will have to pay attention to the payment terms relating to the previous item. Only every two months will some traders send you commissions. Some will not pay you until a minimum of $100 has been generated in commissions. And some won't

pay you unless you make a certain amount of sales first, then wait for some time, and then apply for a payment. Yeah, affiliate services do not return you the money you have won automatically. If you have to ask for it, perhaps it will be a signal to continue to search until you find a good affiliate program.

When selecting good affiliate programs, there are many more things to be looked after, but these are some of the most important. Generally speaking, do your homework and find out precisely how a program operates and find out how many affiliated organizations feel about the system before they waste too much time or money in a tedious way.

GENERATE INCOME ON INTERNET

A vision shared by millions of people allows passive internet profits. This is definitely appealing that you can create a website, offer a service, product, or information, and then sit back and watch the cash flow.

However, developing a passive income is also an issue because it takes perseverance, work, and commitment to make it work. With every person who sits down and watches the cash flow, hundreds of others are still struggling to use their websites.

However, if you start with the best passive income ideas, you can create a consistent flow of profit. Based on good, tested passive income ideas, you will be able to create wealth on the internet for a long time.

The basic principle behind creating a passive income is the search or development of a product or service that can be sold several times over many years. It implies that during that time, the product or service must be attractive.

The best ideas for building a passive income follow. The word "passive" can be a little misleading because any profitable website now and then needs a little research. Yet once you try to create your passive income, the rest will be unaffected if one or more of these suggestions are pursued.

The Blog

By description, blogging must not be called "passive," as new content must be posted regularly. But once you have built your audience, it's quite simple to maintain your website. All you have to do is keep a schedule of new content regularly and answer those who comment. Many popular blogs just require an hour and two of work every day, so during this time, they will raise tens of millions of dollars.

The trick is to choose the best niche or theme that is large enough for many, yet narrow enough to make your blog authority. If you find the right topic to match those extremes, you will have an excellent website for passive income.

Associate Promotion

This may be the most common form of internet investment income. While some might think it is active in the sense that the product or service needs to be marketed, the truth is that many affiliate marketing websites are passive and provide information like blogs or niche sites that appeal to specific groups of people who buy the goods.

The good news is that it almost always doesn't cost any money to start. All you need to do is register on one of the many thousands of websites offering products or services. You earn a commission for every sale, which is usually a small percentage. The more sales you make, of course, the higher your profits.

You may have to choose the desired products to fit your blog, articles, or another kind of website. Once you start, the aim is to increase sufficient consumer traffic to ensure that many customers purchase from their affiliate goods and receive many profits month after month.

Applications

Applications are the multi-billion-dollar company known to everybody using a smartphone. In addition, the development of an app is simpler than ever, although the difficult ones require a design team. If you can come up with and create some fantastic app ideas, you can produce substantial income on a regular basis.

The important thing is the idea. It must be patient, easy to use, and addictive. Games are the most common kinds of applications, but also the costliest. But, if the concept is secure, you can earn significant money year after year from a single first device idea.

Writing of Article

Many websites allow you to publish articles about virtually any topic. For example, Squidoo and Hubpages do not need money or create themselves beyond merely filling out a registration form. You can also sign up for affiliates from sources such as Amazon. The more people you visit, the more money the affiliate products you sell will earn.

However, you will have to write a lot of new and enjoyable articles to make you pay attention. A few hundred to a few thousand dollars a month earn many of the most successful article writers who use the abovementioned sites.

This means that you have to write at least well over 100 articles and probably a lot more to achieve these goals. However, it is possible and does not cost your own money, doing writing for these websites, almost non-brainer. As with other ideas on passive income, your topic is wide enough to reach a large enough audience but narrow enough to be considered a power.

Photography of the stock

Will you want to take photos? If so, you can produce income by downloading your images to one of the many stock websites. When they are deemed good enough, they will appear on these websites, where you receive a small profit for any photograph you accept.

This method takes a while, and many of your pictures may not be selected. But every month you have built up enough stock pictures, you can make a decent profit. If photography is your passion, then this method can work well for you as it does not need the money and can be built over time.

These are some of the great ideas of passive income that you can use over the years to build a healthy income. Recall that the core of passive income is the development of a concept that attracts and regularly sells enough persons.

Active income is income from your current activities, which means you are profits when you are employed. Stop working and no income. The continuous income derived from one-time action is passive income. That means (in theory) that without your actual work, you have money. Passive income is often referred to as residual income.

Terms of financial returns are vague as the principal sense is "all debt payments decrease income." Banks use it to calculate how often money you have to pay future debts. As you can see, this residual income sense has little to do with its other value (passive income). We use the term additional income to avoid any confusion.

Extra money sounds fantastic at first glance. You sit down, and dollars flow into your pockets. Unfortunately, for your income, you will always have to do something. The question is how long you are going to spend on this. Let's look at the example below. You own and rent an apartment. You might argue that renting is an excellent example of passive income without your job. This is not entirely true, however. How about your tenants going to Alaska? You 're going to have to find another. You should, therefore, put some advertising. You can also speak to prospective tenants. What if you need some fixing and painting already when you rent your apartment? You will indeed work for the money, as you see, but it might not take 50 hours a week to do that.

The benefit of passive income is that you have to invest a little time occasionally after an initial effort. That means you can try several passive income transactions. Some of them could bring you significant success. You can also run passive income when working on your current job. On the other hand, you can't work concurrently at two full-time jobs. That means you can only seek to achieve financial success with a small number of full-time jobs in your lifetime. You can, therefore, try a lot more passive income than full-time employment. Some of them could be a great success.

At the end of the day, it is essential to ask yourself: "What am I going to do when I build a solid passive income?" Your reason for creating a passive income could be to do something else. So there is a reasonable question, "What keeps me doing that right now?." After all, we all seek happiness, and work is a third (or a half) of our lives. Why not do things we like most for work?

BASIC PASSIVE INCOME TYPES

Buy and rent an estate

The concept is to purchase and rent a property. If you pay with cash, you only have to keep the property and collect the money from the rent. In addition to the lease, the revenue is generated by the value of the property. Be aware that real estate prices can also be reduced. You may have a disadvantage in that situation. A mortgage can also be used. Then a rent and the monthly mortgage fee must be balanced. Ideally, you could have a positive monthly revenue source.

Machine for sale

The concept behind this form of income is to create somewhere a distributor. This is not entirely passive since you have to "load" your machines with stuff, but only occasionally (for instance, once a month). You will, of course, have to deal with the owner where your setup candy machines.

Build and sell web content

You may put it online as well as earn revenue from the ads if you had something to write about, and that seems to be popular. Cats, athletics, films, education, science, free time could be the subjects.

Sale on eBay

Find and sell a reputable source of certain cheap items via eBay. Your source also could send your customers a delivery.

Write your book

You may not be able to earn a billion, and the idea would be to produce a decent book once and then receive a consistent profit increase. Write and sell an eBook about someone in your field of expertise.

Create a product for software

This is very much like writing a book. Write good software which people want to use, and steady revenue is here. You probably should keep that software, but this is an outstanding opportunity to sell even more new software versions. This probably means you're going to work, but you can also recruit someone to do it.

Dividends and gains in capital

Buy an excellent dividend-paying company. When you invest $200 in a stock today, and after one year, the value is $220, you have won $20 to do nothing. This is again in the capital, and it is entirely passive income.

Income of interest

You can put your money in the savings account, or you can purchase some CDs and earn interest. Visit your bank for more options. Often visit other banks.

Patents, compositions, designs, images.

This is close to the writing of the novel. As a good investor, photographer, or singer, you can earn a little when anyone uses your inventions, songs, or photographs. Let's send a few examples: Edison, Madonna, Pitt.

Delegate the work to everyone else and pay less for your work than you get.

Imagine you're working for $2000 a month. You will not earn 500 $ if you find someone to do your job for 1500$. Your boss does not like this strategy, of course.

Develop and market a commodity

From candies to the space shuttle, a product could be anything. For a start, stay closer to the sweets. Production does not have to be managed by yourself. There are many companies that can do that for you.

Create a company and employ a director

That would, of course, take time. The development of a sustainable company will take many years. But then you are in the passive income zone. Join a manager to replace your job, and you have a passive income here.

Make yourself a renowned social media icon

Social media has become a marketing force, and advertisers take full advantage of the digital environment. The latest survey shows that approximately 75 percent of sales and transactions are achieved in one form or another through social media feedback. In the last few years, even the way we do business and maintain customer relationships has changed dramatically due to social media. A way of selling both online and offline has turned out to almost complete social media selling, from email marketing, telephone calls, networking, and face to face discussion. This does not mean that our conventional marketing strategies are no longer useful or in use, but we use them better by mixing social media marketing knowledge and new practices in order to increase sales through social media.

Increased sales via social media

Selling social media is simple, but it is a tactical way to reach your audience based on demographics and the correct source at the right time according to the most popular social network channel that your local or global audience is using. You can quickly identify potential prospects by correctly using your networks on Twitter, Google+, LinkedIn, and other social networks and then gain insight into your audience's requirements and challenges and use this knowledge. This valuable data will enable you to engage them in a conversation that allows you to email, call, or even meet them in person and offer them your services. It's no news that social media potential helps marketers uncover new sales opportunities and develop existing business relationships that lead to increased sales via social media.

To be successful in social media, you need to plan correctly, put together a clear strategy, spend time, and work hard before you can even think about successful social media sales. Below are some of the best tips each sales representative should follow to succeed in social media.

Set your brand or product and service

Even before you start anything on social media, you must first define your brand, products, and services as a person or group. So, how would you like to be seen as a brand? Do you have the best quality products at the lowest cost or offer the fastest and most efficient services in your niche? Would you like to see your audience as the best team or expert group in a given area? It must all be defined first. In doing so, you will determine how you want your audience to understand yourself and also know the right source of social networking to use.

Create your social media profiles and complete them

After identifying your brand and understanding how you want your public and future customers to be viewed in the media, you will then need to build attractive profiles on all social media channels within your scope. Whether Twitter, Instagram, Facebook, Pinterest, and your LinkedIn profile are created and updated as well. Connect your website to all the above social sites and not to the company page LinkedIn. Make sure your visitors and potential customers don't have any previous information on the pages which will hurt your brand and create controversy. These social media pages are very much representative of your brand, products, and services and must be kept clean and supported by customer-only information.

Identify and follow your target audience

There are many ways to scan the social network for your target audience these days. You can quickly understand what you want, subscriptions, and what you post and show on a regular basis. LinkedIn is another way to search your audience. LinkedIn is an excellent resource for this because its areas, names, different divisions, industries, businesses, and more allow you to search for people in accordance with their demographics. The same can be done with Twitter and Facebook posts updated to specific audiences in order to increase commitment. You can also find your future buyers in the fan pages of your rivals and seek to stain them in ways that we will not talk about if you need more details, email or call the post manager.

Build your social network with your target audience

After knowing who your target audience is on the social networks, start creating your system with everyone you meet by inviting them to share your pages. There are many chances that these people know who you want to sell and make sure that you include all the people in your families, employers, and friends and allow them to share your details with your peers. It will undoubtedly lead you to new members on your pages, and the development will continue. To start this process, make good use of Twitter, Google+, LinkedIn, and Facebook.

Identify the audience's channels

Knowing your target audience's social network platforms regularly helps you focus and bring it to your pages on the same social network channels. You must consider where your target group spends the most time addressing their problems and exchanging details about things that are of concern to them. Once these platforms are identified, join the groups and subscribe to these platforms. There are chances that you can reach many of your target audiences and turn them into fans and subscribers. You 'd rather spend more time on these social networks where the audience spends much of the time. This will lead to more subscribers and potential customers that you will always retain.

Growing sales via social media

Know and track your future customers on these platforms

Tools such as Hootsuite, Tweetdeck, and Google Alerts are a great deal of peace of mind that can help you monitor what your potential clients are talking about online in real-time so that you can respond quickly. Your target audience regularly shares information on websites such as LinkedIn, Facebook, Google+, Twitter, etc. that send messages to their needs and desires. Often only your profile update will test what your needs are. Both of these will give you a clear understanding of how to build and how to target them on social media based on their behavior.

Give objective and relevant content which will inspire and motivate your audience

Now that you have defined your brand, created and enhanced your social media profiles, identified your target group, spent most of your time on the social media platforms, began building your social network and started to find out more about your target population, the next challenge is to provide excellent information about your services, products, and brands. This helps you build trust and become an expert in a specific field. Nowadays, you need to share targeted valuable insights with your prospective customers using various social media platforms in the form of quality content and also to ensure that those contents are forwarded to them at the right time and from the right source.

AGENCY SIGNS ON SOCIAL MEDIA

We often talk to our clients about what social networking can do online and off for their companies. Most of the time, we find they understand that they should use these channels, but they don't know-how.

The value of someone using social media as a useful tool continues to evolve. However, there are still essential concepts related to the use of social media and a website that has emerged in the last few years.

Below are specific ways to tell whether an agency has a good, basic understanding of how social media can be used to drive your website traffic and increase conversions when people are there.

In an existing strategic marketing plan, they use social media as a channel.

Social media should be used as a tool, not a response to the lack of objectives and goals. Your organization will create a social media plan that fits with your current communication content, strategy, and audience. If there's no one, you have more to think about than not getting a Facebook account.

The agency you decide should emphasize social media as a means of marketing and promoting your content and an additional way to get your target audience involved.

Don't you have to post content? Before you start to worry about 5.000 followers on Twitter, focus on figuring out what people want to support you and maybe even become your customer. You probably don't have your logo or the number of times in an hour that you tweet about your solar lawnmowers. You need to build content that will push you to want more. This means that you have more to sell than just a product.

Create sites with shared pages and content.

You know that you want your blog to be "social-mediated," but what does this mean, apart from making sure your URLs work when you post them on Facebook?

First of all, your organization will ensure that all pages on your website are fitted with resources for social media sharing. Not only and page, but only those that your potential customers have listed as pages want to share in their networks with people.

For instance, it would not make sense to include Facebook and Twitter instant sharing widgets on a Terms and Conditions page. But it would be a strategic move to add share tools to a product page. With just one button, your customer could share your product with hundreds of individuals on their network and ask them what they think about it. You wouldn't believe the large proportion of people who depend on their confident systems for advice on everything from purchasing a new camera to moving to another city!

They incorporate feeds and features in social media, if possible.

If you that is there nothing worse to find a virtual waste dump of social media feed, ineffective widgets, and every blog post the company has ever written on the homepage with blinkered light. When you walk through your door, no one wants to see this-trust me. There is a significant difference between an interactive site and an editing lack.

Use good judgment on the homepage and do not bury your main calls for action for a Twitter fan. And while you're there, let them "like" you on your website on Facebook. If you welcomed them, the opportunity is here. Don't release them into the jungle of social media when they arrive. Oddly enough, they can "like" you on Facebook, but if anyone shares a photo on the newsfeed, your customer and your sales are as good as they have been.

What is the solution? Allow symbols of social media subtly famous. There's a center terrain. If someone wants to follow you on Twitter, they will find the icon, even without all the lights, feeds, and arrows that blink.

Your website is highlighted as a home for your entire content.

It specifically concerns the first part of this section. You want all the most critical commitments your customer has to your brand as close as possible to your product. It is not recommended to cultivate a community on an island. You need to create content that returns you to your country-your website.

This depends on the production of valuable content, which people want to press, read, and share. Don't comment on Facebook. Don't comment on Facebook. Blog and market content on your Facebook page from your website. The idea of social media is to use it as an instrument for driving traffic, so you must make your website the ultimate destination for your customers. Consider your website as your Internet marketing plan's Hawaiian. All efforts on your shore should end.

A number of likes or followers don't guarantee you.

I'm not going to try to use the buying friends' example here. You get the picture. If an organization promises a number of lovers or followers for your website, something is wrong. It's one thing to estimate numbers for followers based on advertising and marketing campaigns. It's another thing to sell a bundle of five hundred followers for you without a single advertisement or content. Be cautious. Be careful.

The aim of using social media in marketing is to make meaningful contact with people who want more to your brand than to know when the next selling takes place. It doesn't matter if you have 20 or 7,000 followers if none of them has a message (or your customer), and your efforts are in vain.

We stay up to date with the new social media innovations and trends.

There seems to be a trendy new way every day of using Facebook, Foursquare, YouTube, to get your consumers interested and your brand to market. And these platforms are regularly changing and becoming more robust. All of this means that the agency you choose should be totally enthusiastic about online marketing and how social media can achieve your marketing goals.

And the key is not necessary to know the new trends and innovations, but also whether the social gloves and whistles work for your business or not. At the end of the day, a holistic and comprehensive approach to the use of social media channels is optimal. It can be challenging to tolerate the temptation of browsing social media without a compass, but ultimately your returns will let you know when it will be time to reposition your efforts.

An excellent social media strategy is based on continuous education from available resources and comprehensive knowledge of SEO, the marketing strategy, and the user experience.

CONCLUSION

For society or not to society? It is the topic that many people are curious about. Are all the tweets, comments, and posts valuable? Simply put, yes. You can effectively engage audiences across social networks if you wish to promote your personal blog or launch a corporate Twitter account. This guide will help you understand what SM is and why you need it to communicate with others.

One way to use SM is to connect people, places, and companies who communicate online, from friends to family and colleagues to consumers. As an SM user, you can speak to the like, whether it is another café owner who is adamant about delivering the freshest possible coffee or the consumer who can't get through one more day without the product that you are providing.

More important than ever for individuals and small companies are additional revenue streams. One way to use SM is to extend your message's reach. You are no longer limited to three-state audiences. You will be distributed by SM sites such as Facebook, Twitter, and YouTube from Buffalo to Brussels. SM is how major competitive businesses stay.

Who is social media? What is social media? Consumers use social networks and blogs for reading and posting product reviews, seeking ideas, and connecting to companies. As part of a targeted public campaign, large enterprises that want to maintain a competitive edge will use social media networks.

Do customers rave about your new flavor of muffin? Would customers only be able to get into your club for hours? One way to use SM is to make it easy to express your love in the world, whether it's like your Facebook profile or write a yelp review with your biggest fans.

At the moment, it is the way people and companies choose to collect and share information. Thus, although you think SM has all the strength of a simple band bracelet, there is still a presence here because SM is where you have your customers right now.

Whether you want to start a blog with a seven-year-old mother or to use Twitter to gain insight into your industry, don't wait any longer.

www.ingramcontent.com/pod-product-compliance
Lightning Source LLC
Chambersburg PA
CBHW050009230526
45465CB00003BB/1341